A Miracle

Blessings and Hope of a Polio Survivor
(Romans 8:28)

Steve Clark

ISBN 978-1-0980-7927-7 (paperback)
ISBN 978-1-0980-7928-4 (digital)

Copyright © 2021 by Steve Clark

All rights reserved. No part of this publication may be reproduced, distributed, or transmitted in any form or by any means, including photocopying, recording, or other electronic or mechanical methods without the prior written permission of the publisher. For permission requests, solicit the publisher via the address below.

Christian Faith Publishing, Inc.
832 Park Avenue
Meadville, PA 16335
www.christianfaithpublishing.com

Printed in the United States of America

To our three sons, we wanted you to know God's power is limitless and to know your Grandfather and Grandmother Clark's strength in adversity.

Hope is an anchor of the soul.

Contents

Foreword 9
Acknowledgments 11
1   Summertime 13
2   Strong Parents 18
3   The Diagnosis and Early Days in the Hospital 22
4   Starting Physical Therapy 28
5   Pain Brought Improvement 38
6   Isometric Exercises 41
7   Breathing Exercises 43
8   Fragile Life 47
9   Days Off 52
10 Walking 59
11 Home 64
12 Acceptance 76
13 Pneumonia 87
14 Spiritual Gifts 90
15 Post-Polio Syndrome 92
16 Caregivers 100
Resources 103

FOREWORD

This story is about a child that was never expected to survive polio and the support that his parents and others gave to him through his recovery. But it is also about hope and where that hope comes from.

We trust in hope, and it is who we put our trust in that shapes that hope. We hold on to our training from our homes or our foundations even in uncertain times. As a child, my hope was in my parents and through my parents in God. My parents grounded me at a very early age with a foundation in God and the teachings of the Bible. In the darkest of times, at the bottom of a gray-black lake, God will find you and lift you out of it. If you see good in the most painful situations, that goodwill help sustain you with hope.

As a child, I put what was happening in boxes and only thought about one thing at a time. Having my experiences in boxes gave me the ability to deal with one thing at a time. If I didn't, I believe the severity of everything may have overwhelmed me.

This story is written from the viewpoint of my boxes in my memories—how each box impacted me day-to-day and how it impacted my life because that is how I remembered it and what the poliovirus did to me physically, mentally, and spiritually and how my family and I responded to it. If we see Jesus in everything, our hope is ever-present. We only need to open the door.

God never left my side or my family's side.

Acknowledgments

This book was the result of support from my wife, Connie, who blessed me on a daily basis and encouraged me as the symptoms of polio have returned slowly over the years. She has stood by my side and has served God every day of our marriage.

Chapter 1

Summertime

> Behold, children are a heritage from the Lord;
> The fruit of the womb is a reward.
> —Psalm 127:3 (NKJV)

Summertime in Iowa was a time to enjoy the outside, blue skies, warm summer winds, and green parks with the smell of fresh-cut grass as a family. On one such day, my brother and I could be found with our parents enjoying a picnic with another family of five at McKinley Park, Creston, Iowa, for the Burlington Route railroad picnic. McKinley Park Band Shell hosted many talent shows, concerts, and Fourth of July celebrations during the summer. The Fourth of July fireworks and celebration brought in the entire county to go to the carnival located at the south end of the park.

The railroad picnic was more fun than a reunion picnic because it was so much bigger and there were so many more children. That brought on more games and many more different kinds of food to try. Everyone went home stuffed from eating too much. We would say a quick prayer for everyone at the table, and the family with us would cross themselves before we would start eating. Many families had a special dish that they were known for and brought that to every picnic or family gatherings. Our family was known for their potato salad. A family tradition handed down from Grandmother Clark that Dad and Mom took great pride in. So packed in the ice chest was cold chicken, potato salad, and deviled eggs—the day's menu for us and to be shared with all. As we finished eating, I started to point at my father to make fun of him because he had chicken all over his face. I pointed and giggled as I jumped up from the picnic table and ran off. At the same time, Dad jumped up and started to chase me. We did this every time we were to a reunion picnic, and it had become a family tradition for Dad and me to start the chase. Then, my older brother would join in the chase that would go in random circles with me running and laughing, a deep belly laugh that every parent can remember and love to hear from their child, a true belly laugh of total enjoyment. I had always loved to run and was always laughing with that deep belly laugh. Dad would tell a story of me trying to run a day after I started walking. He would say I was born running and just kept running all the way into high school. My belly laugh would never be heard again, but I would run again, in time.

> Children's children are the crown of the old
> men, and the glory of children is their father.
> —Proverbs 17:6 (NKJV)

Polio was a disease that affected the nervous system to the extent that the muscles could not function and resulted in short-term or long-lasting disabilities in the arms, hands, legs, and feet of many children. Bulbar polio attacked the nervous system that controlled the muscles involved in breathing and swallowing resulting in many children living their lives in an iron lung or death. Children who were placed in the iron lungs because of bulbar polio had a fatality rate of over ninety percent. In a few cases, a child would be infected by both paralysis of the limbs and paralysis of the lungs and throat. I contracted bulbar spinal polio, which meant my entire body was paralyzed to include my lungs and throat. Parents were truly frightened each summer during the polio season for their children. Polio came in waves across Iowa and in the summer through our communities. Towns would shut down public places, parks, playgrounds, movie theaters, and public swimming pools. My brother shared with me that he was afraid of flies and would swat at them or run away from them for fear that they were carrying the poliovirus. At that time, no one knew how the poliovirus was spread, through the air, by an insect, by person-to-person contact, or even in the water. The years 1951 and 1952 were the peaks of the polio epidemic in the state of Iowa. Iron lungs were necessary for the treatment of polio patients with bulbar polio and took constant monitoring by the staff. The children placed in iron lungs had a ten-percent chance of surviving.

Polio seemed to be attacking children more than any other age group in the late '40s and early '50s. Children stayed in the neighborhood and played with a few friends because public places were closed. Bike tag was our number one game during the day and flashlight tag at night. When we could, Annie over would start up but usually stopped because we would lose the ball on a roof. We missed the park but still had fun in the neighborhood. Life went on as people went to work and did the shopping. When the rumors of the disease followed by the newspaper announcement that polio had infected children, people would avoid coming to town. No one knew how the poliovirus spread, and they avoided coming to my childhood home of Creston. Families from the surrounding areas would do their shopping in other communities. Once they learned that polio had indeed been diagnosed in Creston, it resulted in fear for the safety of their children. The homes in town that had children who contracted the poliovirus would have signs posted on their doors that read polio in large letters to help neighbors know where the virus had struck. The fear of polio kept families away from public activities and social events where children would gather, particularly in swimming pools, parks, and playgrounds.

Poliomyelitis—Number of reported cases in the state of Iowa, 1945–1970

1945	320	1953	613	1961	18	1969	1
1946	620	1954	1,445	1962	7	1970	0
1947	176	1955	561	1963	0		
1948	1,236	1956	580	1964	1		
1949	1,217	1957	78	1965	4		

1950	1,399	1958	73	1966	0
1951	466	1959	408	1967	1
1952	3,564	1960	25	1968	1

Source: Iowa Department of Health (1)

This was taken from a special article on polio in The Des Moines Register.

I was one of the numbers added to the peak years of 1951 through 1952. I was hospitalized for many months with an iron lung. The iron lung was this large metal tube that was painted gray or gray green in color. It was mounted on four legs with wheels on each leg allowing the staff to move the iron lungs around. It was large enough to have an adult placed in it, but at Blank Children's Hospital, it was only used for children with bulbar polio. Once placed in the iron lung, you would be fitted around the neck with a seal for the chamber. That seal was a soft leatherlike cone that was snug-fitting or a rubberlike sleeve that helped seal the cylinder. Each iron lung was about chest high for the staff allowing them to care for us without bending over. The metal tube had small windows above each being an access door to allow a doctor or nurse to see when they needed to adjust my IVs or my feeding tube. Each iron lung had a pressure gauge mounted on the top of it to allow the nurses to check the amount of pressure or the degree of the vacuum pressure in the metal tube we were in. Underneath the cylinder, each iron lung had a battery equipped to run the iron lung when we were being moved or in the case of a power failure. It also had a vacuum pump along with an air pressure pump. Each of the devices either removed the air or pumped in additional air to either reduce or increase the air pressure inside the iron lung. You could hear the pumps drawing in the air or forcing it out as you would breathe. In the room I was in, some of us had an additional large oxygen cylinder mounted to the front next to our heads for additional oxygen supply, which I needed at first. I went through intense physical therapy for a year at the hospital and for over six years outside the hospital and at home as an outpatient to overcome many of my physical disabilities. My first two years at home were spent exercising twice a day and returning to the hospital regularly for checkups and therapy that supported what my parents were doing with me at home. The two years of therapy at home by my parents were so beneficial to my overall recovery. My family supported me through extended therapy for the next twelve years to a much lesser degree.

Chapter 2

Strong Parents

> Honor your father and your mother, that your days may
> be long upon the land which the Lord your God is giving you.
> —Exodus 20:12 (NKJV)

This is a story about a mother and a father who were dedicated to helping a son recover from a devastating illness, their strength through that journey, and God's hand in it all.

This picture was taken of my parents about a year or two before the polio outbreak. They were so young for what was to come.

A MIRACLE

Hope was what gave my parents the strength to move forward in our journey. It is also a story of miracles and repeated blessings. God can place people in the lives of others to bless them and influence their lives as they journey down their path. My father was a man who seldom showed his emotions to us or to his friends. My mother wore her emotions on her sleeve but at times was also a very private person when it came to struggles within the family. My mother and father experienced an emotional rollercoaster of being told that their youngest boy had passed away, then he was alive and later he would not survive much longer than a few months, and even later he would only live into his early teens. Yet, through all of this, their strength and determination to see me improve never wavered.

Dad was a drill sergeant who said very little, but when he did, you did what he told you to without asking questions. Many times, he told me I had two choices: (1) to accept how it is and never overcome my physical disabilities or (2) to adapt to and solve the problems so I improve and to truly overcome it. Sometimes, the way he said it was softer: "You can adapt, improvise how you move, and overcome it; you can do it." He would usually work in something about how our family struggle was private and no one was expected to do it for you. He always stressed it was up to me to put in the work to improve.

> Train up a child in the way he should go,
> and when he is old, he will not depart from it.
> —Proverbs 22:6 (NKJV)

Mom and my brother were cheerleaders that would chant that you are strong and you are getting better. At times, I really expected them to pull out the pom-poms. Mom would always stress that the family would get through this and we were never to share how much of a struggle it is or the pain and exhaustion we all were feeling. It was a different time where adults came through the depression and no one was going to help you but family. I was told to never expect or be looking for someone else to fix my problems. Society had a silent feeling that if your family was ill or was going through trials, they were being punished for some wrongdoing in the past. Sins of the older generation would be paid for by the children. This all changed when Jesus paid the price of forgiveness for all the world. The poliovirus was part of a broken world, not punishment. The message was that the family solved their problems and not to expect others to help. My parents both wanted my brother and me to be self-reliant. Another message would come through: that we were taught that hard work would be the answer to your problems and to do as you were told. To this day, I feel hard work will solve many problems, and you don't share physical or emotional problems. That's good and bad, but it was what I needed to succeed in my recovery. At the time, my brother and I didn't see or understand the underlining message, but I now understand what they were doing for recovery. That is why I never really shared this story or talked about the struggles or the pain with others—not even with my wife or sons—and didn't talk about many of the things with my brother. My wife and sons only now are hearing the full story in any detail.

As a child growing up, Sunday was a time to enjoy our friends at church and the church community as we gathered in the church basement for lunch after our church service. Every family brought food for the potluck luncheon; we always brought our family potato salad and some type of Jell-O. You would look for your favorite food from each family and expect them to bring that very same food each Sunday. The children would be disappointed if they didn't. Once we filled our plates and found a place to sit, we waited for the blessing lead by our minister. If it went very long, I would peek to see if we were all bowing our heads and closing our eyes. After the meal, Mom would always talk about the Sunday school lesson on the ride home and ask questions to see if we understood it. Her questions of us did help support the learning points in the lesson, and she would guarantee my brother and me that God had a plan for all of us. She would even ask what Bible verses we were assigned to memorize that morning for the next week.

As a youth, I attended youth groups, Sunday school, church, and special activities of the season. Our church was the center of activity for our family and many friends as we were growing up. Each

Sunday morning, they would ring the bells to remind the community that church services would start during the next hour. Dad always stressed that you have to put your misfortune and in my case disability away or it will dominate your thoughts and your life. So, you don't talk about it to others, and you don't look for help; you simply move forward and adapt to whatever it is so you may overcome it.

What a blessing for me to have parents that truly believed in hard work, self-determination, and trusting in God because this is what was put in my heart. I followed that philosophy and theology without knowing that I was following a belief system of our family and the teachings of our Lord. To honor our father and mother was something you just did because it was best and taught in Sunday school. As a child, I had no idea how much my recovery would be dependent on that belief. Dale Carnegie stressed, "Our thoughts make us what we are."

> When wisdom enters your heart and knowledge is pleasant to your soul, directions will preserve you; understanding will keep you.
> —Proverbs 2:10–11 (NKJV)

Chapter 3

The Diagnosis and Early Days in the Hospital

For we through the Spirit eagerly wait for
the hope of righteousness by faith.
—Galatians 5:5 (NKJV)

He said, this sickness is not onto death, but for the glory of
God, that the Son of God may be glorified through it.
—John 11:4 (NKJV)

My brother and I were excited about going to the picnic at McKinley Park in Creston, Iowa, with all the other families. It was a time when the children could play tag and freeze tag in a large group. We were excited about the day and were looking forward to the picnic. I remember Mom and Dad discussing whether we should go to the railroad picnic at the park that year because the polio epidemic had come to Sioux City, Iowa. Children in Iowa were coming down with polio, and parents were worried about protecting their families. We went because it hadn't broken out in Southwestern Iowa or in our town at that time. We did not know that the hospital in Sioux City had run out of the room because of the large numbers of polio cases that summer. They were also having the highest numbers of polio in Iowa and were seeing an extremely high number of bulbar polio cases in the state for that area. I am sure in hindsight my parents would not have gone to the picnic. No one knew for sure if we were infected at the picnic, but that was the one common gathering place for almost all of the children now infected. It also had brought in families from other smaller neighboring communities that worked for the railroad; cases were now being recorded in them now. Within days of the picnic, polio had arrived in our community. I was running a low-grade fever, feeling very weak with a sore throat, and having trouble with coordination. Because of this, I went to bed early that afternoon and drifted in and out of sleep and not wanting to swallow because it hurt when I did. I woke up with a feeling that I was suffocating, and I couldn't swallow very well. It was the coordination and breathing problem that sent the red flag up. I remember Dad asking me what was wrong with my throat because I was holding my throat. I told him it felt like I swallowed an ice cube and it was stuck in the middle of my throat. It also seemed like the ice cube was getting bigger and bigger. That was another red flag that prompted a call to the doctor. In those days, families called the doctor at home in the evening. I remember seeing my parents on the phone and asking me questions that the doctor was asking: if I could raise my legs; not very well; if I could touch my face, which I could not; and, finally, if I could touch my chin to my chest, which I was unable to. I was even starting to be unable to move my head. The doctor told my parents that he was certain that it was polio and not to go to the local hospital but to get me to Des Moines. I remember Mom and Dad carrying me out of the house. I was told it was a ride to Des Moines to get me admitted to Blank Children's Hospital in Des Moines, Iowa. It was the center for treatment for children with polio at the time. My parents were told that I had bulbar spinal polio. I had become a statistical number of the polio epidemic of 1951–1952 in Iowa. It didn't tell the real story or report that I was in an iron lung or if I had lost the use of arms or legs and to what degree. It just made me a number that frightened the public. The next memory that I had is a lot of people in white rushing around. I was told that at that point, I had lost all ability to move or respond and was barely breathing. I only remember bits and pieces of being placed in the iron lung, but what I do remember was the sound of it swishing and pumping constantly. I remember doctors and nurses constantly peering at me. The iron lung was a large metal tube with glass windows on the sides that worked by changing the air pressure inside the tube. As it removed the air in the tube, the lungs would be filled with air, and then, the air pressure was allowed to increase, which caused the lungs to exhale. It took the place of the muscles in the children's lungs and kept us breathing somewhat naturally. I do remember being able to see through the mirror above my head and that the room was filled with iron lungs and nurses attending to us. Early on, I had no concept of time. What I really remember clearly was thinking, *I just can't catch my breath.*

> He said to them, "Our friend Lazarus sleeps,
> but I go that I may wake him."
> —John 11:11 (NKJV)

The next real memory was a feeling that I was floating on a gray still lake—no sense of sound, no sense of touch, and no sense of anybody or anything being around. This gray flat lake surface was so warm, so comforting, and so pleasant and gave me the sensation of floating on that calm lake surface. The calm was a beautiful secure feeling I felt good about. Then, suddenly, it felt like someone had taken the sides of that calm lake and shoved them together. The calm was shattered with a rough jagged feeling of the surface, and it seemed to hurt. The sound came back, a loud hollow sound that seemed to be far off and echoing. Then, I heard someone say, "He's breathing; get him back in the iron lung." *I believe this was a miracle, and the nurse was placed in the right place at the right time as the instrument of that miracle.* My parents shared with me sometime after I left the hospital that the doctor had pronounced me dead and removed me from the iron lung. A nurse was preparing my body, so my parents could see me after the doctor saw them. It was the nurse who said, "He is breathing," and the doctor who was getting ready to talk to my parents, the same doctor who had pronounced me dead, was the one who said, "Get him back in the iron lung." The pain from breathing was suddenly back, and I was aware they were putting me in an iron lung. I was confused about why I was out of my iron lung and why I did not know I was taken out of my iron lung. The next thing I remember there in the hallway was hearing my parents and the doctor talking about me along with the swishing sound of the iron lung. I was confused again about why we were in the hallway and why my parents were also there in the hallway. I could not see them, but I could hear them talking. I was told that everyone has a defining moment, and this may have been mine. I am sure this moment did influence my entire life—every goal and every decision I did and have made. The doctor told my parents not to get their hopes up and that I probably wouldn't live much longer and that I would have been better off not surviving. I remember one particular statement in the conversation vividly. He said, "Your son will never be anything but a vegetable and will be gone soon," and that made Mom start to cry. I could hear my parents leaving the hallway as they pushed me back in the isolation room with the other children in iron lungs. I remember this because I thought, *You are so wrong, and I can hear you.* This was a gift from God; I heard what was said, understood it, and never forgot it. I was determined to prove him wrong. A tiny seed of rejection can settle in your personality and change things to come; that was God's plan. It was only after my parents shared that story and I in return shared my memory of the gray calm lake that we were able to put the calm gray lake feeling and the doctor pronouncing me dead together. Because of that, we could see that God touched me in that lake and placed that nurse in the hall.

Later, I remember the room with many of us in the iron lungs was in the basement. We were in isolation because they still didn't understand how the poliovirus was spread, and the only way brothers or sisters could see us was to look through the basement windows down into our isolation room. The nurses would position mirrors above our heads so we could see the windows, which was difficult because I could not move my eyes or close my eyelids, let alone move my head. Once they found that out, they used several mirrors so I could see the window. My brother was in the window waving. There was a point that I had improved enough to be removed from the iron lung for short periods of time just to breathe on my own, but because of the inability of my lungs to function, I would be returned to the iron lung exhausted and in pain. That was the start of my therapy for breathing that lasted for a few minutes outside my iron lung.

> For I will restore health to you and heal you
> of your wounds, says the Lord.
> —Jeremiah 30:17 (NKJV)

I was worn out and exhausted and did not want to be removed again because my lungs would hurt and I would feel like I was drowning, but I did it each day. I believe they knew it hurt and was difficult for me. So, they told me it would get better, but they may not have believed what they were saying to me. Again, I remember a discussion that a nurse had with one of the doctors that were treating me as they were standing next to my iron lung. The staff never seemed to realize that I was aware and could hear them when they discussed my progress next to me. I am sure I wasn't showing improvement at the time, so the doctor believed he had to prepare the nurses and my parents for the worst. The nurse was to give my parents an update. The doctor told the nurse that I would never be able to live outside of an iron lung for more than an hour or so each day, and I would probably pass away in my early teens. It was another gift from God, and again, I wanted to yell at him and tell him, "I can hear you, and you are wrong." That tiny seed of rejection again did settle in and change things for me to come, which was God's plan. Each day they would remove me, I would think of what the doctor said. So, I would focus on what they would tell me when I was out of the iron lung—that if I worked at this, I would improve. I wanted to prove the doctor wrong, so I would think about breathing, think about inhaling, think about exhaling, and think about trying to move my chest up and down as I inhaled and exhaled as my respiratory therapist had worked with me on. I would try to draw air in and expand my chest at the same time to increase the amount of air in my lungs. At first, I would get very little air and at the same time would want to cough but could not. Exhaling was even harder; nothing at all would even happen when I tried to exhale and I would have an extremely strong urge to cough but didn't have enough strength in my lungs to be able to cough. In time, I did improve somewhat better, but it was very slow. No matter how small the amount of improvement, I would always have a very sore chest after the work session. The respiratory therapist would repeatedly tell me I had to think about breathing and I would improve. I know that most of the polio kids not in the iron lungs did this without thinking about it. I had to accept that I was part of a bigger plan—God's plan—and that was comforting to me and gave me hope. Our recovery rate depended on our mindset and attitude toward each of us. My breathing did improve, which gave me hope and allowed me to spend more time outside of my iron lung. I now was allowed to go to physical therapy for my arms and legs and then be returned to the iron lung. God's kindness is part of his nature.

> Oh, give thanks to the Lord, for He is good!
> For His mercy endures forever.
> —Psalm 136:1 (NKJV)

As I improved and was able to respond somewhat to the staff, they no longer discussed my progress next to me because now, they understood I could comprehend what they were saying. That probably was a good thing because it kept me from trying to yell at the doctor if he said negative things about my progress. I am sure I would not have been able to yell but I would have tried. Another positive thing that came from the staff not discussing the negative aspects of my progress was that I no longer was tempted to feel like I was never going to improve. From time to time, my improvement would seem to level off and then begin to improve again, which gave me hope. It was so important that we could see our own improvement and our progress.

Chapter 4

Starting Physical Therapy

> Let brotherly love continue.
> —Hebrews 13:1 (NKJV)

Early treatment of infantile paralysis was usually an attempt to revive the loss of function in a limb or multiple limbs. The paralysis was treated with rest and even by placing the paralyzed limbs in casts, which they later found out was not a successful treatment of paralysis. My parents were told that the treatment of casting had not been as successful as they thought, and they were looking for new treatments that would show better results. They were not sure whether it would help or not in my case but knew casting was not very successful and physical therapy was having much better results. The therapy on my limbs could only start after my breathing improved to allow me out of my iron lung. This makes one dependent on the other. My parents chose therapy, which I believe God had a hand in their decision and blessed me with recovery from a diagnosis of less than ten percent would survive.

> If any of you lack wisdom, let him ask of God, who gives to all liberally and without reproach, and it will be given to him.
> —James 1:5 (NKJV)

They had determined that the movement of a damaged limb improved the recovery; thus, many of us went for physical therapy.

My limbs improved, so this meant hot whirlpool treatments before and after they stretched our muscles and moved our joints with force at least twice a day. I remember the first time I saw the tank; it looked like a stock tank on my uncle's farm. Whirlpool treatments before relaxed the muscles and allowed better therapy. The therapist would come in smiling and say, "We are going to the lobster pot, which was a large bubbling whirlpool." They had to plug off my feeding tube before I went into the water each time, but they used a clamp and tape. They would tie three or four of us to the sides and let us bob up and down until we turned beet red. We were also returned to the whirlpool treatment after being exercised and stretched because it helped relieve the pain from the therapy. The pain was real, and it was twice a day every day. The routine of the hospital caused us to lose any concept of time. Hours turned into days, days turned into weeks, and weeks turned into months without us knowing how much time had passed. Each day was the same, and it made it impossible to tell one day from another. This was a good thing for how long we had been there because it kept us from realizing how long it really was. Later on, after we had improved, we did have a few days off and would be allowed to change the routine.

The therapist would move us to the exercise table and apologize to us because they knew this was going to hurt, and it did, but they were slow, careful, and caring. The therapist would tell us that they knew we would have pain from the treatments but that the pain meant we were improving. That reminded me of my parents saying the same thing when I had a very deep cut in my foot that hurt and after a week or so began to hurt even more. The pain worried me enough that I told my parents about the increasing soreness. Mom and Dad told me that the pain was good because it meant the cut was healing. I remember thinking, *Are you really sure about this?* and that same feeling came back when the therapist said it to me. Early on, I still had limited ability to communicate but had regained the ability to move my eyes and my head, which allowed me to see the entire room. You never know how much you miss something like being able to move your head or to move your eyes to see people in the room until you lose it. After the whirlpool treatment, I would be moved immediately to an exercise table, given oxygen, and placed on my back. The first time I was asked to really move my head and even a single finger was the moment that I truly realized how weak I had become and unable to move. Even in my earlier attempt to breathe outside my iron lung hadn't impressed on me how little I was able to do because I had placed it in a single box and only thought about breathing by itself. Now, laying on the table, I was being asked to think about breathing and moving my head and/or a single finger. It was so frustrating and showed me I had so much work ahead of me. It also forced me to think in two boxes at the same time, which was something I hadn't done. I believe I had dealt with things in the hospital by placing them in individual boxes, so I only thought about one thing at a time and had never combined the different treatments and therapy I was going through. This allowed me to deal with the reality of the hospital one box at a time. I am thankful for that because it kept me from being overwhelmed and allowed me to improve. They started by encouraging me to move my fingers and my hands. Sometimes, they would combine that movement or would separate the movement and ask for specific fingers to be moved. The therapist would then massage my hands and physically move the joints of my fingers and wrists and then repeatedly ask me to move my fingers and hands without their help. If we couldn't move a joint, the therapist would move it for us. As I progressed, they would ask me to raise my hand and forearm. At first, this was impossible, but in time, I learned to raise my hand and forearm. Then, they progressed to my entire arm. Once I could lift my arm, they ask me to reach across my chest and hold that position. We worked on the right side and the left side of my hands and arms, and in every case, I found my right side responded much sooner and much stronger. This same process was repeated in my feet and legs with a new twist in which I would be asked to bend my knee and hold that position. Then, the request came to roll my knees to the opposite side of my body. I was learning how to roll over. Something an infant learned on his own.

> In the multitude of my anxieties within me,
> Your comforts delight my soul.
> —Psalm 94:19 (NKJV)

They started with easy movements of my head. They would ask me to turn my head to the right or left and touch my chin to my chest. Again, I found that my right side was much stronger and quicker to learn how to turn, but eventually, I accomplished the task although my left side responded slower and more painfully. Therapy was an endless task of attempting to move my joints after they stretched and massaged them. God will do many great things in our lives if we have the patience and wisdom to wait for it and to see it when it happens.

As I became more proficient in basic movements, they would eventually add resistance to the movement by holding my hand or my arm with their hand. I never really progressed to using weights in the hospital. I don't believe the doctors ever truly believed that I would ever be able to work with weights because of the severity of my bulbar polio. I came much further than they ever expected I could. My parents were never really given much hope for me, but they continued to believe that I could. My resistance to the exercises was the therapist pushing against the movement with their hands. Once I was able to do all the movements that would be required of me to be released from the hospital for outpatient treatment, I would be closer to going home. I knew this and worked so hard to achieve it so I could go home and see my family. It was difficult to only see my parents and my brother through a window, and that was maybe once a week. Therapy for my spinal muscles consisted of being placed in a sitting position and asked to turn my chest completely to the right or left. I also was asked to lean forward and straighten back up to an upright sitting position. My early attempt of leaning forward resulted in me literally falling forward and being pulled back up by the therapist to the upright position. I couldn't fall out of my chair because I was belted in to keep me from falling out. Falling forward and not being able to return to the upright position was because I didn't have the strength to sit back up. The therapist soon realized that I enjoyed this sensation of falling forward, so he would place his hand in front of my chest before he would ask me to lean forward. Another exercise that was done sitting in my wheelchair was trying to arch my back; this sounds simple, but at first, it was not. However, I didn't mind it as much because it only made my back sore and it was not painful. Again, in time, I was able to accomplish the tasks.

> Rejoice always. Pray without ceasing. In everything, give thanks; for this is the will of God in Christ Jesus for you.
> —1 Thessalonians 5:16–18 (NKJV)

As the large muscle groups began to improve, we started working on the smaller muscle groups that allowed me to twist and turn. I would be asked to rotate my hand or my arm inward and outward. This rotation would be repeated in my neck, chest, hips, and legs. Improvement took longer than the larger muscles that allowed flexing at a joint, but it meant real improvement. You never wanted not to be improving because it meant you wouldn't go home soon. Improvement was so very important for those of us that were still being returned to our iron lungs; if we didn't improve, it meant that we may never go home. At times, I wanted to ask why me, but hope was always present in my life. We also worked on facial exercises and even eye exercises each day. This didn't hurt, but my left side never seemed to improve. My face would droop, and I had to work on smiling, wrinkling my nose, and raising my eyebrows; it sounds simple, but I was slow on results. The right side of my face came back much sooner than my left side, so I had a lopsided smile. I still cannot raise my left eyebrow or wrinkle the left side of my nose, and my smile is a little off too. I stayed with the facial exercises up through college at night in my dorm room. A good friend came into my dorm room and found me making faces at myself in the mirror. He almost left without saying anything. We had a good laugh, and I explained what I was doing and why. I had to show him I couldn't raise my left eyebrow or completely close my left eye. I was still slightly unable to totally smile on my left side, before he realized I never regained these functions. He was the first person I ever shared that with and one of the very few I ever did. This led us into a long discussion of polio and what I went through as a young child. Two years later, I had to talk about my facial paralysis. I had met a young lady that was studying speech pathology in an anatomy class. She had done a short-term paper on damage to the facial nerves resulting from traumatic injuries and how it changed speech. She had noticed my left eye and my smile and questioned me if I had ever been in a car accident. We talked about the speech therapy that I received early on in the hospital and what I had gone through because of the paralysis of my face.

By the third grade, the paralysis of the left side of my face was not so evident but still slightly lopsided. Therapy to improve my facial expression was a daily part of my life and would be for several years.
Even though I continued therapy exercises into college, I still have never regained total control of the left side of my face.

When I first came home and just before I was released to go home, I was asked to color in coloring books. I was mad about being given coloring books until I actually tried it. Coloring was a fine motor skill, and I had great difficulty even holding the crayons, let alone staying in the lines. I was very slow at first, but this too improved rapidly. I never admitted to my friends I spent time coloring at home after school. Mom even got her a coloring book and colored it with me at the kitchen table. I still wanted to use weights or the tennis ball to help my hands, but the coloring was better for me. My coloring time moved to paint by number painting, which I enjoyed. It was a therapy extension of the coloring book, which meant no more crayons and no more coloring books. The other plus to it was that my friends could see me painting and never knew it was the therapy. Mom loved the paintings because she knew the story behind them and what it really meant to my improvement. Again, she painted too; she even framed a couple of my paintings. Another activity that helped improve my hand movement was putting together different sizes of nuts and bolts. I had to be able to pick them up and rotate the nut to get it on, which was very difficult at first but later on became extremely easy as I improved. Dad put me to work on his workbench sorting and putting nuts with bolts together in jars. He would use me as an assistant when he fixed things around the house or barn. I love spending time with Dad and becoming somewhat of a handyman. Another job my brother and I had was to water all our plants in the yard. We used water from the pump and carried it in buckets to the plants. We both thought we had way too many flowers around the house and in the garden, but it was good for us.

Mowing the lawn was another chore that I had to talk to my parents into allowing me to try. Mom and Dad finally agreed and assigned me to mow just the front yard because it was level enough to for me to walk on. It was much more difficult than I had expected because the push mower used all my body to push it and made me shake before I finished doing that portion of the yard. Not only did it teach responsibility that we had to do the watering and mowing without being told, but also it strengthened us both physically. Because Dad worked on the train crews, he would be out of town for two or three days, so we were expected to take care of the chores without being told to—just do the work and take pride in what you did. Both Mom and Dad would say, "If a job is worth doing, it is worth doing right," and they really did mean it! Mom would use me in the kitchen much the same way Dad would, and she would try to keep my hands busy with anything that would make me use my fingers as a form of exercising. Cutting, chopping, and mixing were top of the list for me to do.

 Polio also caused problems with my eyes' ability to adjust or follow movement. In the hospital, I would be taken to an inside room with no windows and asked to follow a flashlight beam on the wall—up and down, side to side, and even in circles, which was a hoot because it made me dizzy and I would be unable to stay with it for any length of time. I kept doing my eye-tracking exercises up to my tenth-grade year in high school, and it helped some. I would follow the lines in my room up and down in the corners of the room and up and over the door. I later found out that I had a reading problem because of my weak muscles in my eyes. The next surprise was that my entire right side came back faster than my left side—right arm, right leg, right hand, and the entire right side. I stress that because this was new, you see I was left-handed before polio, and after polio, I had to work on being right-handed because my left side was so weak. Try switching hands the next time you print something. This added to the frustration when I went back to school. I had to learn to print all over again, and I was a very slow reader now. In one of my early grades, my teacher would push my hand away as I followed the words with my fingers when I was called on to read in class or during silent reading time. She told me repeatedly I was a lazy reader and needed to pay closer attention when I was reading. She wasn't being mean; she was doing what was accepted in education at the time to correct slow readers. My reading problem was because I would get lost on the page when I would read due to the weak eye muscles. They jerked, and I would find myself looking at another line on the page or looking at a word in the next sentence. I didn't know something was wrong because I thought everyone had that problem and I just had to work at it harder and it would improve. I didn't know, and the teachers didn't know. I never complained because in my mind, I had nothing to complain about. I simply would read a section two or three times to get all the facts of the story or section. Each time I would reread a section, I would pick up new facts I missed the first time. I really did think everyone had to read like that to get all the facts. This reading problem was never really diagnosed until I was in graduate school at the University of Nebraska, years later, in a learning readiness class by that teacher. The class was designed to teach us to identify reading problems and how to correct or support the child in learning. She gave me lifelong skills that summer that would improve my reading comprehension and help speed up my reading. It was also the information I used as a teacher and that same information I shared with some reading teachers later as a school administrator.

> Oh, give thanks to the Lord, for he is good!
> For His mercy endures forever.
> —Psalm 107:1 (NKJV)

I also had to adapt to a problem with my dominant eye and dominant hand. Most people have their dominant eye on the same side as their dominant hand. I was left-handed before I was affected by the poliovirus, which meant my dominant eye was on my left side. Because I developed faster on my right side of my body, my favorite hand became my right hand given that I have a dominant eye on the left side and a dominant hand on the right side. This caused problems for me when I threw a ball or when I shot a basketball or any other hand-eye coordination skills that I never really truly overcame. To this day, I now do somethings right-handed and a few things left-handed because of my dominant eye. Therapy was never ending from one to the next all day long—breathing, limb, facial, and swallowing therapy—each day and blood tests every morning. The routine, day after day, was mind-numbing, and that caused a loss of concept in time for us because the days were all the same. This struggle to read left me with a better understanding of learning disabilities and gave me a desire to help and support children when they struggled in school. God's timing is perfect. He blessed me with this understanding so I could help others. I believe later in my life, as a teacher, I was looking for students that were uncomfortable with learning because of my past experiences. I tried to understand each student's struggles

A MIRACLE

with learning and their learning styles. When I taught biology, I hope I had empathy for those students that struggled to understand the textbook because of my past. As a school administrator, I tried to be supportive of our special needs program again because of my experiences at reading comprehension in my early years of education. Past experiences give understanding and shape all of us.

> Wisdom is with aged men and, with length of days, understanding.
> —Job 12:12 (NKJV)

Chapter 5

Pain Brought Improvement

> So you shall serve the Lord your God,
> and He will bless your bread and your water.
> And I will take sickness away from the midst of you.
> —Exodus 23:25 (NKJV)

The therapists told us that we would have pain from the work sessions of physical therapy, and the pain meant we were improving. They couldn't tell us how much pain or how long the pain would last because it was different for each of us depending on the amount of damage from the lack of movement or the amount of nerve damage.

God made an amazing machine called the human body that could deal with the damage caused by polio. Part of that machine is the nervous system and the muscular system along with a warning system to them that is called pain. Pain tells the human body there is a problem or to just slow down and be careful. Pain from my polio was long-lasting because the nervous system had no longer stimulated the muscle or sent any message to the muscles that stimulated any functions. That lack of any functioning caused the muscles to shrink and shrivel up. The muscles then became rigid and very stiff from the lack of use. The tendons and ligaments shrank and became very tight and unable to stretch or react. Tendons and ligaments attach bone to bone or muscle to bone and allow the human body to move at the joints. The physical therapy would massage and stretch the muscles

A MIRACLE

along with the ligaments and tendons so they could move again as God had designed them to do. As therapists did this, they would cause slight tears in the tissue resulting in pain, but they were very good at keeping the pain at a level we could tolerate and the tears to a minimum. When the muscles are damaged, they collect fluid that protects the muscle and carries off damaged cells that cause swelling, and that results in pain. Because I had to develop my breathing before I worked on movement, I had a greater degree of damage due to inactivity. The therapy caused pain in the muscle tissue and in the tendon and ligament tissue at the same time.

The pain was constant and made many of us want to quit, and some did because it was so intense. Eventually, the tissue would respond in many children, and that also helped the nerves to reeducate and muscle memory to return along with neural pathways or lines of communication from the brain to the muscles. Then, the nerves can develop new lines to communicate to the muscles and began to stimulate the muscles. It is truly amazing how God designed our bodies. The new lines of communication would cause the muscles to now start to function. Once this happens, the muscles would start to use energy as they worked to move. This process caused waste products to build up in the muscles and again pain. In time, the muscles would get better at getting rid of the waste products and reducing that pain. So, the whole process caused pain for all of us, so we recovered at different rates and different degrees. The skill of the therapists was to change the exercises each day to allow the different muscle groups time to repair. So, the therapists would develop the workouts around a different muscle group to stretch and exercise each day. The muscle improvement was directly related to the amount of damage polio did to the nerves and how well the body was able to develop the old communication pathways to the muscles or to develop new pathways of communications.

The greater the damage was, the harder the recovery was, but it did happen for us. God made this amazing machine called the human body that can be repaired from within if we understand it and work with it. We all had to live with pain that was constant and would make us want to stop and accept the present as it was. There are different levels of pain: one was the pain that was with us constantly and tended to numb us from what was going on; the other was so severe that it would cause us to become so disoriented that we would not be able to respond to exercises and would need to stop exercising. The really sad thing is that in some cases, it didn't matter how much pain the children went through; there was no improvement for them at all. The pain was such a part of our lives going through therapy. If we had a day that the pain wasn't so bad, we thought something was wrong. For some of us, the pain would follow us at different degrees even into the night, and the next morning, we really wanted to get to the whirlpool to relieve it before we started in again. Pain was always present during the after physical therapy. It was also very present and painful at first when working on breathing. Exhaling was the hardest and would cause my entire chest to be sore after the work session. I experienced extreme pain in my legs and hips at first when I attempted to walk. Even my feet and ankles would hurt early on. Walking involved so many large and small muscles that had to work together. It took time to regain the ability to walk. Isometric exercises were nothing more than slight soreness and eventually subsided completely. Therapy at home brought with it mild pain and at times intense pain that subsided during the first two years of exercise at home. I was so blessed. I did improve in time at the hospital and even to a much greater degree at home with the support of my family.

> Be of good courage, And He shall strengthen your heart, All you who hope in the Lord.
> —Psalm 31:24 (NKJV)

Chapter 6

Isometric Exercises

> But He knows the way that I take; When He has tested me, I shall come forth as gold.
>
> —Job 23:10

Isometric exercise was another form of physical therapy that allowed me to work on my large muscle groups in my arms and legs during the day at school. I was shown new techniques by a therapist from the hospital who first had me work on my legs by placing my foot on the outside of the chair leg and pushing in and then placing my foot on the inside of the chair leg and pushing out. I would alternate my right leg and my left leg and get a pretty good workout during a single class. When the bell rang, I could now go to my next class and work on my arms by hooking my arm under the desk and pushing up and then could alternate and place my arm on top of the desk and push down. I found that I could hook my arm on the inside of the desk and push out. That would work on a different group of muscles in my arms. I also could work on my spinal muscles by arching my back and locking or holding my muscles in that position for ten to twenty seconds and relax and repeat the process. The pain of exercising had gone away slowly in the fifth and sixth grades and was replaced with sore muscles that lasted all day. The soreness would be more intense in the morning and lessen throughout the day. In the tenth or eleventh grade, even the soreness went away finally. I felt normal for the first time in years as I went through my daily activities.

One day, in my high school chemistry class, I cracked the desk during a lecture while exercising my left arm. The chemistry instructor heard the popping sound and asked me to talk to him after class but was understanding when I apologized and told him what I was doing. He told me he didn't know anything about me having polio and said, "Please don't work out quite so hard in the future, or I may have to ask you to pay for the desk." He smiled and laughed and said, "If you need to break another one, go for it." I never pushed that hard on the desk again in his class. In junior high school and high school, I did my exercises with Mom supervising from time to time and in my room on my own with Mom's ever-present watchful eye. When I went to college, I no longer had the luxury of having my mother give me her look if I forgot to do my workouts. Dad would just ask as to when I planned to work out—tomorrow or the next day—and add, "You need to pay the price, so better get to it." In college, I could use the weight room, along with isometrics that gave me many workouts that were part of my life. Exercising no longer felt like it was therapy but just what I wanted to do and what I enjoyed. I looked at any challenge of my life through the lens of polio. I believe hard work and setting goals would answer most any problem that I encountered. I even looked at my academics and Bible study through that lens.

> For what man knows the things of a man except the spirit of the man which is in him. Even so, no one knows the things of God except the spirit of God.
> —1 Corinthians 2:11 (NKJV)

Chapter 7

Breathing Exercises

The Lord is good, a stronghold in the day of trouble;
And He knows those who trust in Him.
—Nahum 1:7 (NKJV)

I remember the first therapist that would work with me on inhaling and exhaling because he kept stressing I needed to think about breathing, and he was so very right. Breathing therapy was another area of exercises that I placed in its own separate box by itself. Each time the therapist would come to work with me on my breathing, I only thought about what we were doing at the moment and shut out all other activities of the day. I never tried to think about the entire day or the activities that I went through each day. I simply concentrated on the moment and the energy it took to be successful at that time. The early exercises were simply breathing outside of my iron lung and thinking about breathing deeper. This would hurt as I tried to breathe, and the pain would last even when I returned to my iron lung. Our goal was to remain out of the iron lung longer and longer each week; I did it in time.

Later, as I improved, we worked on improving and increasing my ability to breathe with some force. My lungs were so weak at first that I could not even move a thin strip of paper in front of my mouth. The therapist would place that thin strip of paper that was about a half-inch wide and two inches long directly in front of my mouth by holding part of it on my chin, so the other end of the paper extended up to my mouth just in front of my lips. He would instruct me to inhale and exhale in an attempt to move the paper strip. At first, I could not do it, not even a vibration, but again, in time, as I learned to exhale with more force, I did. He would hold a mirror up so I could see the vibrations as I inhaled and or exhaled. Even the slightest movement was pointed out at first. We had a big celebration the first time I could move it when I inhaled and exhaled.

As I improved, I also worked on swallowing each day—sometimes at the start of the exercises and sometimes at the end of the exercises. I was blessed to see improvement and thankful because I had to improve in breathing to be able to work on all other areas of my disability. I was thankful for any improvement in even if it was slow at times.

> I will praise you, O Lord with my whole heart; I will tell of all Your marvelous works.
> —Psalm 9:1 (NJKV)

Exhaling was a real challenge for the therapist. They would tell me I had to get the used air—carbon dioxide—to make room for the new air, oxygen, into my lungs. I would become dizzy doing this because of the lack of oxygen to my body but that improved too. I never wanted to cough when I was outside of my iron lung working on breathing because I could become so dizzy due to the lack of oxygen from the coughing even though the cough was so very slight. The coughing never gave you time to inhale to replace the oxygen. I could never lose my concentration on breathing in and out because I simply would not breathe deep enough unless I thought about it and again would start to get dizzy. After my lungs became stronger and the dizziness went away, the therapist would hold a match about three inches in front of my lips and had me work at blowing it out. The first time I got it to go out, I cheated and inhaled. I know he knew what I did, but he still celebrated it. The therapists who worked with us who had been in the iron lungs for extended periods of time on breathing problems were the ones who were so strong

A MIRACLE

and positive with us even though they were working with the high-risk children. We were the ones that only had a ten-percent chance of surviving. They saw so few of us improve and had to witness the decline in so many. It had to be so stressful and difficult for them to keep positive, but they did. I owe so much to them for my positive attitude and recovery. My next major improvement came when the doctors removed my feeding tube because my swallowing had finally improved. I now could drink liquids and try very soft foods such as Jell-O, Jell-O, and more Jell-O. No ice cream at all, as it would cause my throat to restrict because of the cold and hinder swallowing. I wanted to eat ice cream and peanut butter, which was absolutely not allowed.

Somewhere in the process, we graduated to the second and third floors of the hospital and left the basement. Those of us that had paralysis of our lungs still used oxygen at first and returned to our iron lung for short periods of time each day. It was easy to pick out the kids that had lungs that were affected; we had a bluish-gray tint on ourselves, while the other kids who had paralysis of a limb or limbs had a pink tint to their skin. We, the bluish-gray ones, were a little jealous of the pink kids. I remember, one of the first days in my new room, I was lying in bed and breathing with my oxygen mask, which was all I could do, but I could look around the room and move my head slightly. A boy in a wheelchair came in, looked at me, and said, "Hide this." He had a package of play money that we were not allowed to have anything from outside of the hospital because they were worried that it could bring an infection into the children's wards. Still being mostly paralyzed and unable to even talk yet or move with any success, I simply looked at him. He said to me, "Oh, you are one of them." He wheeled over next to the bed, lifted up my head, and put the play money under it. As he left the room, he turned around and smiled and said, "Don't tell anybody." He laughed and said, "I will be back." A few minutes later, a nurse came in to ask if anyone had been in the room. Then, she realized that I couldn't respond and left. He returned, smiled at me, and said, "Thanks for not telling on me" with a large grin. He took his play money from under my head and left. He started visiting my room every day and would talk even though I couldn't respond. He would tell me about his day and about what he was going to do when he went home. His big thing was to go back to church when he got home. I didn't have enough wind power in my lungs to speak. Your vocal cords need to have air passing over them to allow a vibration that makes sounds and words. We had some great one-sided conversions in my room. I guess it was because I was a good listener. Kids can be so great at times.

> By this, we know that we love the children of God, when we love God and keep his commandments.
> —1 John 5:2 (NJKV)

I wish I could have known him after we left the hospital so I would have been able to tell his parents how caring he was to me. I wish I could have attended his church with him to tell them how he treated me and what it meant to me.

Chapter 8

Fragile Life

> All flesh is as grass, and all the glory of man as the
> flower of the grass. The grass withers, and its flower falls
> away, but the word of the Lord endures forever.
> —1 Peter 1:24–25 (NKJV)

None of us knew or were really aware of how easily life could be taken away. At first, some of the children would ask where one of us went without any celebration and would never really get an answer. When we did, they would say they were just moved to another floor. I never ask at first because I couldn't communicate, and when I could talk, I understood, so I didn't ask about it. This was something I just put in a box and didn't open it ever. I have only now talked about it.

> As for man, his days are like grass, as a flower
> of the field, so he flourishes. For the wind passes
> over it, and it is gone, and its place remembers it
> no more.
> —Psalms 103:15–16 (NKJV)

I learned, and I adjusted but never really was able to put away the uneasiness of not waking up, or seeing the empty bed that was stripped down with the lingering odor of bleach in the morning. Most of us understood that it meant another one of us had passed away. The nurses never discussed anything about the children that didn't make it. They tried to keep it from us, but we could see the empty beds. Beds became empty for two reasons: We improved enough and were sent home, or we would die and never go home. Now, if one of us improved to the point that we were released to go home, there would be a celebration. Usually, you would see the nurses very positive, smiling and telling each of us that a patient was improving and would soon go home. They usually tried to tell us we too would improve and go home. Parents normally picked up their children about midday, and you would get to see a small parade of smiling nurses and therapists escorting them down the hall. That was so cool, and it did give us hope. The other reason for an empty bed, usually there in the morning, stripped down so that all you saw was the plastic cover on the mattress and the smell of bleach in the room was, as I learned, that one of us had died. Someone passing away seemed to always happen at night or when we were asleep. In the morning, at first, we seemed to lose someone every couple of days. It did scare me to the point early on that I really didn't want to go to sleep. I wanted to hide but couldn't hide from the empty beds in the morning or what it meant to all of us trying to recover in our iron lungs. My worst memory was watching another polio victim pass away and not being able to do anything or even call out for help. It was early in the morning, and we had just finished getting our IVs checked and adjusted along with replacing my feeding tube. I was awake and alert because of the morning activity for me and others in the room when I saw the older boy next to me looking empty and scared. Fear has a distinct and devastating look in the face of a child. That look is very real, and you will know it when you see it even for the very first time. He was also becoming very quickly light gray in color. I had seen the color change before but never that fast along with that look of total fear. His face suddenly seemed to change from fear to being totally blank. I knew he was in trouble, but I couldn't call out for help, so I wanted to hide, but I couldn't, and he was gone. It was only a moment and so fast, but for me, it seemed so long. The nurses were only gone for a moment, and he was gone at that moment. I didn't even know his name, but I did know he was in an iron lung just like mine and I could be gone just as fast. The nurses gathered around him, and that blocked our vision of him and what they were doing. With very little discussion between the doctor and the nurses, they immediately wheeled him out without removing him from the iron lung leaving an empty space next to me. Visions of that look of fear will always be with me and the memory of that desire to hide from what was happening. I never talked about that day, not even with my parents. I put it in a box and tried not to open it but did each time I would see an empty bed in the morning stripped down with the smell of bleach in the room. I am sure my father understood this feeling—the best of anyone in the family because he found his father in the barn after his father had passed away. He had to tell his mother, brothers, and sisters that their father was gone. He never talked about that, and it was Mom that told me about it when I was in high school along with instructions to never ask Dad about it. I never did. God strengthens us, and when I learned his strength, not mine, I gained hope. That hope would see me through each day, and I would improve.

    The other children that had paralysis of one or more limbs usually went home before those of us that had been in the iron lungs. Our survival rate was less than ten percent. We were the ones that were blue gray in color and usually worked with a therapist on breathing and attempting to talk. We also knew that we were the ones that weren't expected to ever go home. Some of the children, I believe, just gave up. Children usually are so positive and never give up, but this was different for some of them.

    The therapists were the ones that got to know us personally. They could see even the small positive changes and would give us daily encouragement and describe the improvement to us. They were the ones that picked up on any movement and to what degree it improved. They also saw the pain we went through to make that improvement day after day. I was determined not to be someone who never went home. I believe that was the major factor in wanting to work through the pain of therapy. At first, in your fingers and hands and then in your arms and legs, the pain would last right up to the next therapy session. Each morning, you would wake up with your hands and arms stiff and unable to even open up your fingers, but by the end of the day, the therapist had your arms and legs straight and your hands open by massaging and stretching them daily. After many sessions, they started me moving with resistance. I would try to close my hand with a washcloth placed on my fingers. Early on, the weight of the washcloth was too much to close my hand, but soon, I was able to close my hand with the therapist pushing against it. I know they would fake it and act like they were pushing really, really hard and they would definitely fake it when they acted that they couldn't hold me back. Fatigue would set in, and my hands would shake as would my arms or legs when the muscles had enough. The pain in my lungs never really went away. It would wear me down from breathing each day even up to the day I left the hospital. The pain and the inability to improve caused some of the children who were treated in the iron lungs to quit or stop trying. I was always taken to the hot tubs with the same children, and we were the ones that needed to be submerged up to our chins because we were struggling with breathing problems. I was paralyzed from my head down so they would submerge me no matter what.

Friendships were made between us because we were struggling with breathing problems. Betty Ann had lost the use of her arms and was a bulbar polio patient but had the use of her feet and legs. She could draw with her feet and even print words with her feet. Her lungs were weak, and she had difficulty talking but had a great smile. Every day, she would greet us with that smile as we were placed in the hot tubs. She was released before me but never regained the use of her arms and still had to return to the iron lung. I found out later she passed away at home. Ben, another bulbar polio patient, was my roommate for a time. I believe we were roommates because we both were working on our speech and they hoped we would be encouraged to talk to each other when we went back to our rooms. Ben missed his sister and his dog at home the most. He always had his dog as a companion because it slept with him before he got sick. It worked; we did talk some, but Ben always ran out of air in his lungs to talk for more than a few sentences. We both turned gray or blue when we talked too much, so we could tell the other one, "Talk to you at speech." He started not talking and then not going to speak at all. One morning, his bed was empty, stripped down with the smell of bleach. I really did think of Betty Ann and Ben as friends.

> Precious in the sight of the Lord is the death of his saints.
> —Psalm 116:15 (NKJV)

Many of us were old enough to understand that death was a real possibility, and even if we went home, our lives may never return to normal. Hope can come from so many sources such as a child's prayer taught to me by my parents when I was very young. The prayer was "Now, I lay me down to sleep. If I die before I wake, I pray to God my soul to keep. Amen." I remember praying this simple child's prayer many times before I slept. I also remember reciting the Lord's Prayer, which I learned at church. As children, we learned the reality of knowing someone that had passed away too soon, but a simple child's prayer that had been forgotten brought peace. Children are so amazing because they are normally positive and supportive of each other no matter what they are going through in their lives.

> Happy is he who has the God of Jacob for his help, whose hope is in the Lord of God.
> —Psalm 146:5 (NKJV)

Chapter 9

Days Off

> Come to Me, all you who labor and are heavy
> laden, and I will give you rest.
> —Matthew 11:28 (NKJV)

Dad was so proud of the progress I had made and that I would be going home soon. He wanted to know everything I had done and how the activities in the hospital were helping. Days off only came after we were able to leave our iron lungs for extended periods of time and to move somewhat on our own. They tried to do things that didn't seem like it was therapy but was still an activity to help us improve.

One day, we were allowed to try to move down the hall in our wheelchairs without help. If we made it, we got to use one of the new wheelchairs for the next two days. It sounds easy, but I had a very hard time even gripping the wheels to move them. So, I adapted by using my forearms to move the wheels. I also was stronger on my left side, so I kept turning into the wall, and they would have to reline me so I could start back down the hall. The first few times I tried, I never made it down the hall without having my arms and hands shaking so bad I had to stop. That is when they gave me the rubber ball to keep with me and squeeze so I could improve on the strength in my hands. I kept that ball with me and took it everywhere. As my grip improved, I got much faster and was able to control my wheelchair.

A MIRACLE

In time, I was able to win the new wheelchair for two or three days. That rubber ball was a hand exercise I kept doing into junior high school. We called them wheelchair races, but a turtle could have beat us down the hall. The real goal was to just make it all the way down the hall and for me to stay in a straight line. I also had to stop using my forearms and start always using my hands.

> The light of the eyes rejoices the heart, and
> a good report makes the bones healthy.
> —Proverbs 15:30 (NKJV)

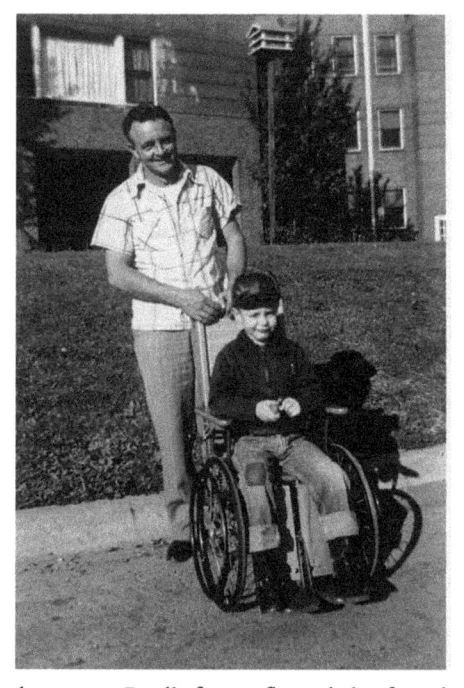

The smile on my Dad's face reflected the fact that I was nearing release from the hospital. I could open my right hand and exercise it with a rubber ball on my own. My left hand still needed a therapist to open it and move it.

One day, those of us that were able to sit up in wheelchairs, instead of going to therapy in the morning, were wheeled out on a balcony, and the only thing we were told was that we were going to do something different. It was sunny and clear, and we could see part of Des Moines down below us. For many of us, this was the first time we had been allowed to skip therapy and even go outside. We all thought this was so cool and thought they just wanted us to have an opportunity to go outside and see the blue sky and get some fresh air. One nurse got excited and said, "Everybody, look up." A few of us needed help to move our heads up, but we all got there. Then, you heard airplanes coming right over our heads, and as they did, they wiggled, dipping their wings from side to side. I don't know how many planes flew over, but it seemed like it went forever one after another. We were later told the Air National Guard wanted to show their support for us and would do this from time to time. They did it two or three times while I was in the hospital. We had to work twice as hard that night to get through therapy, but it was worth it. Another day that was different was when the nurses let some of us go down the hallway in our wheelchairs on our own. For those of us that made it all the way down the hallway, they told us we could have chocolate milk. Now, you need to understand that some of us had trouble swallowing because of bulbar polio and the thick chocolate milk just would not go down, so that made it a no-no, but it was a treat. I was one of the ones that couldn't swallow the chocolate milk. The young nurse that gave it to us felt so guilty. She should never have felt this way because she was so good with all of us children. Finally, one of the therapists said that was good that we tried, even though it made a mess gurgling out, but even that was fun because we broke the routine.

Now, some of us were moved to small rooms upstairs that had one or two roommates in them. We found new activities and new exercises. The majority of children were in large bays of six to eight patients or more of all boys or all girls. I later realized that the large bay areas were children that had been paralyzed in their extremities, while the smaller rooms were exclusively children with bulbar polio and were receiving breathing treatments in the iron lung and/or breathing therapy. I believe that also had a secondary purpose to protect other children from two things: First, they still had concerns about spreading any kind of infections to those of us with bulbar polio and what it would do to our recovery. The second was to lessen the knowledge that many of the bulbar polio patients did not survive. The bay-area children did not see the empty beds resulting from death. Visits by our parents at first were only through the windows—the second-floor windows in my case and many others. That meant the parents were using ladders to get to our windows. That didn't soak in until just after I was allowed to go to the window in my wheelchair. Dad was the first one to wave at me through the window and ask me how I was doing from the other side of the glass. That was because the hospital was not allowed to open the windows for fear of any infection; I had to turn my wheelchair sideways, so I was next to the glass to hear Dad's question. Dad was aware that I had difficulty talking, so he usually asked questions that only took a no or yes answer. Mom did make it up the ladder a couple of times to see me but simply waved and told me she loved me. I know she was never comfortable on that ladder because she had a fear of heights, but still climbed the ladder to see me with Dad's help. When it was time for us to go home, our parents were allowed to meet the parade at the main entrance only. My brother had to stand outside the doors. Children from the outside were not to have any contact at all with the children inside the hospital. The hospital staff were worried about what we might be exposed to or could pass an illness from the outside on to each other. Even though my brother may have been immune to polio at that point, they worried about colds, mumps, measles, chicken pox, and other childhood diseases and what that would do to our recovery. At that time, vaccines had not been developed for any childhood diseases. Children would become infected with a disease and would be quarantined at home to stop the spread of each disease. The other children in the family usually became infected when one member would get sick. Doctors made home visits to support what the parents were doing to reduce the spread of the disease. Sometimes, my brother would be in one room, and I would be in another room. Warning signs would be posted on the doors to our homes with the name of the disease to let the neighborhood know.

I contracted the mumps and was quarantined at home. I had a mild case but did have both sides of my neck infected resulting in swollen glands. My brother was infected at the same time but only on one side of his neck. Dad and Mom allowed us to play on the front porch but never left our home. I am sure I dressed myself because I have a "Popeye the sailor" hat, a cowboy shirt, and pants on. I posed for the picture in front of the house standing next to the sign declaring the mumps. My brother wouldn't let anyone take his picture with his swollen glands.

Mom insisted on taking my picture by the mumps sign
by the front door.

Hospitalization and separation always bring a feeling of fear and sadness to the ones involved in it. Polio brought that to both the children and the parents. When we talked about missing each other and/or the fear, it helped each of us to cope with the fear of polio. It helped to be able to see each other and to talk to each other even with a window between us.

A MIRACLE

Family and friends were not allowed to enter the hospital to visit the children. Parents would gather at the windows outside to wave and give support to the children. A few parents brought ladders to see their children on the second floor. It was difficult to be separated from your family, but the doctors and nurses were very supportive. We were never alone because the hospital staff became our foster parents. I am sure that was rewarding when we improved but so sad when they watched some of the children never really improve or others pass away.

I was so isolated at first because I could not communicate with anyone, so I was left with my thoughts: thoughts of death, but I did have prayers I had memorized as a very young child; thoughts of being left alone, but I had another polio patient that talked to me for weeks when I could not be part of our conversation; and thoughts of being abandoned by my family, but I had the window that I could see my parents through. Some of the children became depressed and would withdraw, while others became angry, so they lashed out at everyone. We did not have any counselors or ministers that visited because we were isolated due to the fear of being exposed to the poliovirus. I had a few Bible verses I remembered that comforted me and Sunday school memories that did come back to me in my isolation. I could and did remember the great family times in the church basement at gatherings. I was so blessed to have the Holy Spirit in my thoughts and God guiding others to answer my needs. It was so important to see my parents and my brother through the windows.

> If then you were raised with Christ, seek those things which are above, which Christ is, sitting at the right hand of God. Set your mind on things above, not on things on the earth.
> —Colossians 3:1–2 (NKJV)

Schoolwork could have helped us with the feelings of isolation during our hospitalization. Many of the children that could have been able to study or have some kind of support would never have had the time to do it. That was because the physical therapy and other treatments were too time-consuming to allow schoolwork. So, many of us were too sick to have been able to do any schoolwork at all, and as we recovered, the schedule did not allow us to focus on anything other than our recovery. The children that were in the hospital for a very short time and returned home were simply placed back in their class and expected to catch up with support from their parents and teachers. I lost an entire year of school. Hospitals and schools had little or no coordination through the polio epidemic because so little was known about the threat of the disease. The schools were more focused on keeping the buildings clean to reduce any spread of the poliovirus and whether they would allow a student to return to school or remain in their home with in-home tutoring. When school officials were assured that we would not pass the disease to other children or adults, they began to develop plans on how to better support the children during hospitalization and at home. Many children returning to their homes at first were physically unable to attend school. This was due to buildings not having ramps or elevators for children that could not utilize stairs and/or even sit in the student desks. The polio epidemic encouraged schools nationwide to better facilitate handicapped students' needs. It also brought to the attention of educators the need to modify instructional techniques for learning disabilities in children. Many of the techniques used in today's special education classrooms were the result of what we learned during the many years of polio's after effect and a blessing for children to come. When you live with God as your guidepost, things will change, but you may not see it unless you look for his influence.

Chapter 10

Walking

> He will not cry out, nor raise His voice, nor cause
> His voice to be heard in the street.
> —Isaiah 42:2

All the therapy that I had been through up to this point would also support or directly was related to being able to walk. The physical therapy work to my arms and shoulders that allowed me to use my arm would also allow me to stabilize myself when using the parallel bars as I would attempt to walk. Lower-body exercises in the hip, legs, and ankles also related directly to walking. The therapist had worked with me moving my legs from my hips because my early attempt at walking would be swinging my legs forward from the hip because my legs would be in braces and I would be unable to move my knees. The coordination and strength to move my lower leg was lacking. I had to work at strengthening my ankles by pushing my foot down against resistance and raising my foot up against resistance. This simulated stepping and pushing back up as you walk forward. I worked at bending my knees from different positions—first laying on my back and later sitting on the edge of the exercise table by raising my lower leg and returning it against resistance. This also simulated moving forward in a stepping action.

As I accomplished each skill of walking, I was getting closer to actually being able to attempt walking. The physical therapist told me they appreciated the way I set goals at all of our skills but cautioned me to look at walking more moderately when I set a goal now. We started with being placed in the standing position with help, but my legs would wobble and just collapse. I got somewhat better but always needed help to stand until I was told to stretch up with my legs, and it worked! To explain this, take your hand, stretch it open, and then try to strengthen it even more and keep stretching; now, hold it. That was what I did to my legs to stand. It worked; it was exhausting to maintain for very long, but it worked. I now needed to lift my knee while stretching my leg. When it was too difficult to do both, we went to the parallel bars and braces to walk.

Now, part of my workout was to spend time standing by stretching to improve how I stood and to get stronger and better at it. They weren't sure if I would ever be able to stand and lift my knees alone but kept me working at it while also working on walking with braces.

My first day at the parallel bars with my braces locked in place was mostly standing and adjusting my braces to my leg. I was told my goal for the day was to be able to swing my legs forward one or two times per each leg. They placed me between the parallel bars while one therapist held me up; the other one adjusted the bars to just below my armpits and next to my chest on both sides. They explained this would allow my arms and shoulders to develop as I worked with my legs. They were right. The first attempt at swinging my right leg forward was first explained that I would need to shift my weight to my left leg and rotate my right leg forward as I picked it up from the floor. Both therapists took hold of me and shifted my weight to my left leg and rotated my leg forward so I could feel what the action was. Then, they repeated the action by helping me slightly. Each time we repeated this, they would attempt to help me less and less; this was painful. After I learned to rotate a leg, they put the movements together, and I attempted to rotate first the right leg and then the left leg in a coordinated movement. This skill took me three to four weeks of daily therapy to take three steps before I wore out. I was so excited and happy over just a few steps.

I started setting goals and trying one more step each day. I was so determined to advance, but for many weeks, I didn't get that

A MIRACLE

one more step. As I learned to rotate and swing my leg forward, I also had to plant my foot in a stable position to maintain balance. Accomplishing the movement of my foot and stabilizing it was the most difficult skill in attempting to walk. Now, I needed to think about how to shift my weight, rotate my leg, and plant my foot just to take one step. This was complicated for me, and I needed to concentrate on each of the new skills.

At first, I was so intent on learning to move my legs forward and stabilize my foot that I actually forgot to breathe, so I became light-headed and the therapist reminded me to exhale with more force. I wasn't very good at multitasking at that time, but necessity is a great teacher.

In the hospital, before I left, I worked at walking to the end of the parallel bars, turning around, and walking back. In the next phase of walking, they allowed me to unlock my braces at the knee, try to pick up my leg and swing it straight forward, and plant my foot. This was much harder and took much longer. Once I was allowed to walk forward by bending my knees and demonstrating that I could maintain my balance, we took the leg braces off and started over again without braces. The same process that we did with braces we did without braces. A new blessing was that the pain involved in moving my legs was now mostly extremely sore muscles when I attempted to walk and would be relieved by the whirlpool treatment.

The simplest movement had to be relearned through sore muscles, repetition, and hard work, but in time, we all did improve at different rates. I remember one of the older girls was determined to learn to walk again before her new baby brother did. All of us encouraged each other and were so happy with any improvement that we celebrated as a group at times.

> I can do all things through Christ who strengthens me.
> —Philippians 4:13 (NKJV)

Prior to leaving the hospital, I was able to take about fourteen small steps without braces between the parallel bars, down to the end of the bars, turn, and come back. I could also walk across the room with braces and crutches without assistance. It was a busy room—some of us walking without braces and some of us with braces. In one corner were steps with handrails on both sides; it too had someone on it. I worked on the steps only after I learned to walk with my braces in the unlocked position. All of us were so weak and exhausted when we walked into the room without help; we wobbled, and our steps were so small, but it was walking. I would shake for some time after walking. Going across the room hurt so bad, but I never admitted that to the hospital staff. I only told them it made me sore. I just wanted to go home. When I was released to go home, the goal was to use the braces and crutches at first and advance to walking without assistance. I was so fortunate that I had the summer to work on walking without crutches or braces before school started. That time working with Mom at home made the difference. I improved rapidly at home using my crutches without braces, then using furniture as a small child would as I walked, and finally walking like any other child in my school.

> Jesus said to him, "Rise, take up your bed, and walk." And immediately, the man was made whole, took up his bed, and walked.
> —John 5:8–9 (NKJV)

Being able to start on weight as my resistance when I exercised first at the hospital on weekly visits and then at home improved my endurance and strength. I still had ups and downs as I improved. My muscles would tighten and not allow me to bend my knees, and we would have to reduce the amount of weight I was using to exercise with and start over again. I would return to stretching and less weights or stretching alone for a week. The phone calls Mom made to the therapist at the hospital when this happened would always have the question "Should he continue exercising?" I always had hanging over me the expectation that I was done improving. The discussion then ended with the decision to continue a week or two more, and if I regressed, then we would know to stop. I had advanced

A MIRACLE

past what anyone at the hospital had expected. Mom would readjust the exercises, and Dad would reset the pulley and ropes for me. My first two years went like that four or five times a year; then, my progress was steady and fast. The setbacks were gone, and I could see real improvement in my ability to walk. I was walking with a slight limp in my left leg. My limp improved over time until it completely went away. I was never expected to even live or later even live outside of my iron lung, but now, I was walking. What a blessing to have improved that much! I can never thank the staff at Blank Children's Hospital and my parents enough.

> And my God shall supply all your needs
> according to His riches in glory by Christ Jesus.
> —Philippians 4:19 (NKJV)

Chapter 11

Home

> The Lord will give strength to His people; The
> Lord will bless His people with peace.
> —Psalm 29:11 (NKJV)

I did improve, and then, they started to talk about going home. I was able to be in the parade down the hallway with the doctors and nurses all encouraging me and wishing me good luck. Many of the other children would come to the hallway to be part of the well-wishing. I knew being able to go home was good for all of us to see because when I saw it, it gave me hope that I could go home too. Some of the kids made cards for me in therapy and handed them to me as I passed them in the hall. I wanted to push myself out, but the nurses always did wheel us to the doors. Only at the doors did they let me wheel myself out through the doors. I know I had a smile so wide as I left the hospital under my own power. I talked too much and ran out of air telling the other children I would come and wave at them when they left. I was out of air when I greeted Mom and Dad, and I could not even tell my brother I was glad to see him. I was wheezing when I tried to talk, so I stopped. I was so excited about going home, to be with my family, to see my friends, but most of all to not see the empty beds in the morning. That vision of empty beds would be with me for some time, but now, my hope was renewed, and I felt secure and safe for the first time in a long time being at home.

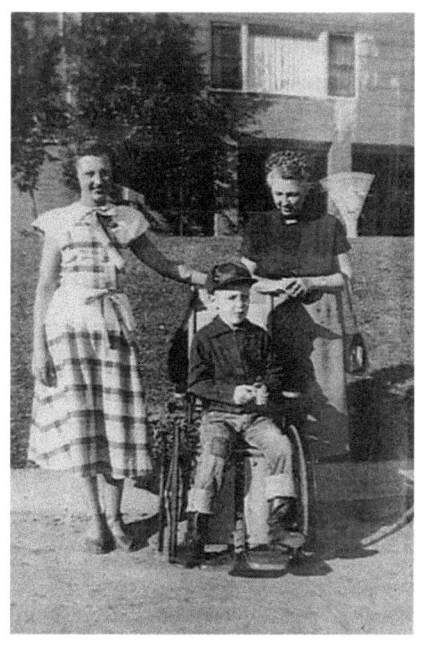

My mother and grandmother are pictured with me the same day that Dad was there at the hospital. I still had problems opening my hands but was getting better. I was still wearing my leg braces under my blue jeans.

That was not my best smile, but that was getting better each day.

Before going home, Mom had instructions on how to wake me at night and pat me on the back to encourage breathing. Mom was expected to watch my breathing and do this each night as needed. Mom's first night would never be forgotten because she was not aware that I slept with my eyes open and how low my breathing would go. That night, she entered the room to check on me and found me lying very still, so still that she thought I wasn't breathing. She had always been able to hear me breathe during the day because I had a slight whistle to my breathing. Mom and Dad had never been around me at night in the hospital as they were not allowed in the hospital. During the night, my breathing would become so shallow that you couldn't hear it or see any movement of my chest. The very shallow breathing did not have that whistle that I had in the daytime. Mom expected to hear me breathing; she couldn't, and that set off her alarms. My eyes were also open, and only the whites of my eyes were visible. She saw a motionless child not breathing with the whites of his eyes showing. That would have scared any adult walking into my room. I woke to her screaming for Dad. After that, she knew what to expect, and I was gently shaken awake for my treatments, but the screaming did work as a great alarm clock and woke me up. I still marvel at my parents' strength to support me—what a blessing. Another blessing came from the struggle; it gave my Dad back a stronger faith, and it grounded my mother in her faith. It strengthened the faith of my parents through adversity and made them stronger.

> And we know that all things work together for good to those who love God, to those who are called according to His purpose.
> —Romans 8:28 (NKJV)

Dad was private in his faith and strongly believed his worship time was to be kept in his prayer closet. Mom made sure my brother and I went to church each Sunday and were active in our youth groups. Things at home were changed to adapt to my handicaps. My bed was a wood platform that Dad built, with a thin mat on it and no pillow. He also built it lower to the floor so it was easier for me to get in and out of the bed by myself. The doctors were worried about my developing spine and wanted to keep it from any curves forming. They wanted me flat and on a hard surface at night. The room had to be made for me to move around without falling, so the furniture was moved to accommodate the path of my wheelchair if I needed it. The doctors did not know if I would improve or start to decline as many did when they went home. I refused to use the wheelchair unless I was exhausted. I improved fast and graduated to crutches, even faster in walking without them. My improvement was the results of Mom and Dad doing in-home physical therapy twice a day, every day with me. I only had a few setbacks—four or five times a year for the first

A MIRACLE

two years. The setbacks only lasted for a week or so, and I would start improving again.

Going home was great because I got to see Mom's and Dad's friends and sometimes their children. I say sometimes because many parents were still afraid to have their children around me, not knowing if I was contagious or not. The polio vaccine was still two or three years away, and the polio season still came back to Iowa communities each summer. My brother was believed to be immune because the medical community felt he had contracted polio but only ran a high temperature and had muscle pain or soreness for two or three days. Less than twelve percent had mild symptoms as he did. We both were on opposite ends of the poliovirus percent. Again, what a blessing for our family that only one of us had to be hospitalized with complete paralysis and a prognosis of never surviving. I can't imagine what that would have done to my parents if we both had been hospitalized with paralysis. My brother had to make adjustments also as I was the family's focus, and he did. He was my cheerleader when I did my exercises and would help Mom change my weights as I went through my daily workout in the evenings. I rapidly improved and could walk short distances without crutches. My strength and skill to walk without crutches got much better at first in the house and a few weeks later in the yard at home, quickly no longer even needing the crutches. This was a goal because I wanted to go to school without the crutches. Many of my parents' close friends would allow their children to visit with me at home because Mom and Dad had assured them that I was no longer contagious.

My brother David and I were pictured with his cat. At this point, I was always wanting to go everywhere with him, and he put up with me, but I am sure I was a pest to him.

    For four long years, I am sure Dave had to make me the center of the family's attention, and he did. Now, I was a tagalong for my brother, and when he had a friend, I wanted to be part of that too. He still was a big brother, and I know he would have rather played with his friends without me but put up with his little brother. After I was released from Blank Children's Hospital in Des Moines, Iowa, to go home, I still traveled back and forth to the hospital for outpatient physical therapy. This was the first time I used weights as resistance in place of the physical therapist pushing against my movements by hand. This was much harder for me to do and very exhausting.

    I was scheduled for outpatient treatments twice a week at first, and in time, the therapy sessions and doctor checkups were moved to once a week and then every other week. With less and less therapy, I started to show very little improvement in my strength and/or flexibility, which was expected for me because of the severity of what I had been through. My breathing was now getting better, and I could blow up a balloon when we worked on improving my lung capacity at the hospital and home. Breathing exercises would be with me over the long term growing up.

A MIRACLE

At home, most of what I needed to improve my breathing was exhaling with force and increasing the duration of exhaling. Dad would play games with me to see how long we could exhale together or who could blow up a balloon the fastest. He always won but would be so silly looking doing it. I was able to beat Mom when Dad was at work, but I think she really didn't try that hard. This game we played was difficult for me, but that utilized the muscles involved in breathing, and it did help tremendously over time.

In the hospital, I worked on swallowing water in larger and larger amounts and then Jell-O that tasted better but filled me up so fast. Eating was a new problem for me and my parents. I wanted to eat like everyone else, but when I would try a new food, I usually choked on it when I tried to swallow. At times, the choking and gagging were severe enough to really scare my parents and me. I always told them it was okay, but it did scare me. So, I would go back to soft food and liquids. Mom and Dad thought of a new way to help me improve, so they made very thick and chewy Jell-O. The chewy Jell-O worked and really helped me improve on swallowing without choking a lot. The hospital started using chewy Jell-O with me too. At first, everything had to be pureed, but in time, I could eat small amounts of solid foods. I improved slowly, but it was something that no one at school knew because I could hide it by being a picky eater. I would tell the teacher I was feeling sick and wanted to sit in the office to rest so I didn't have to go to lunch. I always felt better after lunch, so I really think my teachers knew but played along. I really loved it when we had soup or anything mashed that went down easy. I never wanted any of the kids to see me choking.

I improved over the next two years and could eat almost anything by the sixth grade just carefully and slowly depending on what it was. The summer of my sixth-grade year was my first attempt to eat ice cream. Ice cream had been considered off-limits for me to eat because the cold would restrict my throat and hinder my ability to swallow. We were at a picnic where dessert was homemade ice cream by one of the other families. Everyone but me was given servings of ice cream by my mother. I understood that but felt left out, so I did the typical thing a sixth-grade boy would do by pleading with my mother to let me try a small serving. I think she gave in because of the look on my face and the fact that I had not had ice cream since before I went to the hospital. I found out that day that I could eat ice cream in very small quantities although it did restrict my throat slightly. I could drink water without any ice after the ice cream, and that would help me swallow. Over the years, I have gotten better at eating ice cream, but I am very careful to not eat too much or too fast because it will indeed restrict my throat to the point where I have trouble swallowing. Eating those few spoonfuls of ice cream made my day at the picnic. To this day, I do not drink any liquids with ice in it because I have just gotten used to no ice in my drinks. If I do, I still can feel my swallowing becoming more difficult.

Another milestone in my off-limits food was Christmas Day during my seventh-grade year. After opening my presents early that morning, Mom and Dad offered to serve up anything we wanted for breakfast. I am sure they thought it would be a typical breakfast item, which it was for my brother. I requested a peanut butter sandwich that Mom absolutely refused to give to me, and Dad took on the role of defending my request and said to let me try. Mom disappeared into the kitchen in somewhat of a huff and reappeared a few minutes later with one piece of bread with a thick layer of butter and a thin layer of peanut butter. Without saying a word, she handed me the peanut butter slice of bread and stood there staring at me. I took two bites from the bread, and Mom took it back and said, "Not another bite until you swallow those." I had to swallow very hard to get the bites down, and Dad immediately handed me a glass of water to help get it down. It worked I believe because the sandwich was mostly butter and the water helped with the swallowing, but it still made my Christmas Day to have a peanut butter sandwich. I have been very cautious my entire life with peanut butter sandwiches.

After being released from the hospital to go home, I returned for therapy and checkups twice a week at first. As I stabilized, the visits went to once a week for my therapy and checkups in the hospital physical therapy facility. The trips to the hospital were time-consuming, to and from the hospital, because it was about seventy-five miles one way. At times, our appointment would be pushed back until the therapists were done with children at the hospital who needed additional time for their therapy. We were normally scheduled first thing in the morning, and if they needed to reschedule us, they would put us later in the afternoon. Mom and Dad tried to make that trip more than just the drudgery of therapy by allowing me to visit the Iowa State Capitol building, and each time, we would see a different part of the building. A few times, legislators would introduce themselves to us and normally would have supportive things to say about my condition. At first, we always took the crutches in case I would have to walk very far. This would cause the legislators some concern when they saw me. They would stand back because they didn't want to cause me to fall but still very supportive and polite. In a very short time, I was able to walk without the crutches, so the visits became more comfortable for them and me. I am sure they had the same concerns as others about possibly catching the disease, but the trips to the Capitol became something that some of my parent's friends wanted their children to go to the Capitol with us. Mom became somewhat of a tour guide for my friends that went with us from time to time. My brother would help as a guide and loved the trips to the Iowa State Capital building. He always encouraged us to climb the stairs to the top of the capitol. In time, we could do just that.

My parents were advised to accept that I was done improving. Even with the addition of small amounts of weights in my exercises, the hospital saw very little improvement. We were to accept my physical inability and understand I was only able to do so much. My parents openly and absolutely disagreed with that concept. So, my mother became my daily therapist at home. She and Dad planned to give me all the exercises that I was getting in the hospital now at home. Dad built an exercise table designed almost identical to the one at the hospital. Mom had studied how the weighted exercise bags were made from leather and filled with sand. She designed weights from old blue-jeaned legs by sewing the legs into bags and filling them with sand to hold during the exercises or to sling over my ankles, much the same as they did in the hospital. At first, I was unable to lift the empty bags, but that improved dramatically as I was receiving therapy from my mother twice a day—in the morning before school and in the evening after school. I now was receiving fourteen to sixteen hours a week of exercises as compared to one session a week at the hospital. I still went to the hospital once a week and later once every two weeks for therapy and checkups.

With me exercising at home, now, my parents saw the pain firsthand and felt my pain with me as I worked on the exercises at home. I am sure the doctors were trying to prepare my parents for what they believed was the outcome of my disease. The physical therapists were the ones who were very positive about working with my parents and coaching my mother. Mom would regularly call one of the therapists and ask for guidance on how to work with a particular muscle group or secondary muscles that allowed rotation in my extremities. I have no idea who this man was, but I know our family owes him so much for my recovery. God blesses people sometimes by placing the right person in the right place at the right time.

The first few times I exercised at home, my brother told me that he realized how weak I was for the very first time when he saw that I could not pick up an empty weight bag with my hand or lift the same empty bag with my legs. That bag weighed about two pounds or less empty with the buckles on it. Later, when Mom started exercises at home, she was a never-ending taskmaster and showed very little sympathy when I wore out or did not reach the goals she set for the month. My Dad would look at the heavier weight that Mom had already sewed and asked me when I was going to get to them. He would push me for an answer and then just smile and leave. I remember one month when I didn't improve enough to change the amount of weight that I was working with. He looked at me and told me that it was my responsibility to improve and to get with it. Mom stayed in constant contact with the therapist changing the routine and the type of exercises she used. Dad was always able to adjust the table to mount pulleys and ropes and tell me that only a wimp needed a pulley. He would smile and place his hand on my shoulder. He almost always would rub my head and smile when he would call me a wimp as he was leaving the room. I had lost the pain of exercising in the fifth or sixth grade and replaced it with soreness in my muscles during the day as I improved. I was able to make it up the first flight of stairs in the Capitol building by the fifth grade. I know I was blessed to have parents that were determined to help me improve and not accept the status quo.

The oral vaccine came first; it was given to us in school by county and city health workers. We lined up by classes and one by one stepped up to watch a nurse place two drops of a reddish-color liquid on a sugar cube. We gladly took it and enjoyed the sugar. I am sure that sugar was used because the vaccine was nasty tasting. Many children were successfully tested in Dr. Salk's early trial nationwide. Many health-care workers also volunteer to be part of the trials. In 1962, Dr. Sabin's vaccine was given by injection. Both were successful and started a rapid decline in polio cases. When we would go back to the hospital for follow-up doctor and therapy sessions, the other children were amazed that I was still working twice a day at home. Many of them had parents that couldn't be involved in at home exercises and had been convinced their children would never improve. I was proud of my improvement and proud of my parents for their determination. Going home also let other polio kids from my home town see each other, and that was so cool; there is strength in numbers, and it gave us all hope.

After the first year at home, a new form of therapy came into my life swimming, which would be a blessing and later in my journey an even larger blessing that would give direction to my life. The therapist recommended swimming as an exercise that would support my body weight and exercise a large number of muscles at the same time, so my parents put me in Red Cross swimming lessons. I advanced through the classes rapidly and became an instructor's aid and later an instructor at the city swimming pool. I am sure it had a great deal of influence on my rapid improvement and my love of swimming. I was encouraged to join the city competitive swimming team that resulted in reminding me I was still recovering from polio. I was forever being reminded I was different than the other children. We had to have conferences with the doctors for permission to participate in competitive swimming. The physical therapists felt that it was a good idea. The doctors worried about the stress that it would have on my lungs and heart but decided I could participate if

I would allow them to give me regular checkups and be attentive to any problems that might arise with my heart or lungs. I realized early on that this was the chance to prove I was like any other child and enjoyed the competition of swimming. I also wanted to prove that I could do anything any other child could do. Swimming was such a major part of my life growing up and contributed so much to my physical improvement. I know that at times, I wanted to ask why me when I would experience setbacks in my health or strength. I had to trust in him and his plan.

> But I will hope continually and will praise
> You yet more and more.
> —Psalm 71:14 (NKJV)

When I asked my parents the question "Why me?" I always got the answer that God was at my side and God blessed me with the right people in my life to help me through everything. When I would push for a deeper answer as to why I survived, Mom and Dad would answer that God has a plan for all of us and he was not done yet. Later on, in high school, my Dad asked the same question of the doctors at the hospital when we were in Des Moines for my checkup. They were expressing how far I had come and how the work at home had helped with my improvement. That is when Dad questioned, "Why Steven?" I feel Dad asked that question for me, and he wanted me to hear what the medical people thought so I could accept better why I survived and not others. The doctor and the physical therapist were in agreement that they felt because I was raised in an environment that taught me to honor my father and mother and respect the wisdom of the elders had much to do with my improvement. They also felt that the training coming from both the home and our church allowed me to trust in my parents when they told me that hard work would result in me improving. The physical therapist stressed that they felt the respect that I had for adults made a major difference during my therapy—again because I trusted in their wisdom and what they told me to do during therapy. They added that the early intervention of physical therapy had to help in my recovery and the fact that I was a healthy individual with a strong heart were factors in my recovery. Dad followed up, "Why did Steven survive?" The doctor said, "Sometimes, there is no medical answer to why someone survives, and in Steven's case, that is true. He was in a group of cases that had less than ten-percent chance of living and even less than that to improve. The only answer may be God, and his case is one of those." I believe Dad had asked each of those questions before, but he wanted me to be present to hear the answer. I still ask myself from time to time why me. I was so blessed to have had Christian training at a very early age that guided my family and me through my recovery.

Chapter 12

Acceptance

> This is My commandment, that you love
> one another as I have loved you.
> —John 15:11 (NKJV)

I wasn't prepared for my first outing downtown to the shoe store for new shoes in my second week at home. I still had leg braces and used crutches to walk, but I was walking and excited about new shoes. I was soon able to cease using the crutches and braces something I was so very pleased about. Dad had parked the car as close as he could, and we were only two stores away. As we walked by the JCPenney store, the five and dime store to get to Brown's Shoe Fit, we went down the sidewalk, and I saw a mother and her son were looking at us and not moving, but then, the mother pulled the boy by the hand to the other side of the street. She was afraid to be around us for fear they could become sick with polio. Once in the store, another family also left in a hurry. Dad explained to me the fear and assured me everyone would learn that I wasn't contagious in time. The workers in the store were super and really nice as they helped us pick out my new shoes.

As I returned to school, I was the target of some teasing by two boys and three girls early on. The girls would start with name-calling and laughing that started the boys pushing me and asking me why I didn't try to stop it. I couldn't; I was too weak and too uncoor-

A MIRACLE

dinated. The memory of the taunting at times left me angry and unable to trust the children in my school. That uneasiness to trust other children stayed with me for some time because I had expected the teasing to come back, and I never knew who I could trust not to participate in the teasing. The actual taunting went away by the time I was in fourth grade. Those children turned out to be very good friends, and I valued their friendship.

Mom always told me to ignore it, and it would stop when they found out it didn't bother me. She always encouraged me, and in time, the name-calling by the girls did go away. Dad, on the other hand, would give me a look of disgusting disapproval followed with, "What's the matter? Can't you take it?" He would follow that with some slap fighting with me. When he slapped me, he would show me how to block the incoming slap, and if I didn't slap back, he would slap me more and a little harder. In time, I got the message; I was to defend myself by blocking the pushing and in the case of a few boys by pushing back. I did this, and the pushing went away. I learned later as we became very good friends that they were somewhat afraid of me as I was different. A few of the parents in town thought that I and other polio children should not have been allowed back in school.

> This is My commandment that you love
> one another as I have loved you.
> —John 15:12 (NKJV)

I found out a year after my return to school that the school board and some parents had a discussion about allowing the polio kids back in school. The school board had done their work and talked with the doctors at our local hospital and Blank Children's Hospital. The school board was assured we were not contagious and not a threat to other children or the teachers. It wasn't just me as we had other community and railroad children that had been in the hospital for polio: A boy who was ahead of me in school had a leg that never totally recovered, so he walked with a limp, and a girl in my high school class that lost the ability to lift up her foot because her lower leg was atrophied. We became very good friends, and they were some of the few students that knew I had been hospitalized in an iron lung. There were two other older kids that returned to school too.

Attitudes changed as the town learned we would not pass along polio to them and as our outward disabilities were no longer really viable. All of the children that had conditions that were visible went through the same thing at first; it just took time. Looking back on how I appeared to others was funny and scary. I had a limp when I walked and a droopy left side of my face, even my left eyelid was droopy, and I had coordination problems eating at lunchtime. I would miss my mouth when trying to eat; that went away in the first few months at school. I would run out of air when I talked; that improved the first year back in school. I'm not sure how my teacher felt about that, but I'm sure it was with mixed emotions.

Years later, that little boy who loved to run and laugh had come so far. I approached athletics with the same attitude as I did physical therapy. In high school, I was on the school athletic teams of football, basketball, and track and the city swimming team. Swimming and track were my best and the ones I really enjoyed. As an eighth grader, the high school coach had me working out from time to time with the high school track team so I could run with or beat some of the high school runners. I ran the 440-yard dash, now the 400meter dash, and the 220-yard dash—again, now, the 200-meter dash—and anchored the mile relay team all through school. From time to time, I anchored the mile medley relay. The members of that track team were and are friends for life. My middle school coach and high school coach were so supportive of my love of running, but only my mother and father knew the price we paid as a family for my success in track and swimming. The therapy had also turned into working out to improve my strength for running and in swimming competitions. I had two goals: to keep improving from the problems of polio and to keep gaining strength for athletics. The hours of physical therapy assisted and directed by my mother and father at home changed everything for me and strengthened my belief that God had his hand in my recovery and my success in athletics. God uses people in this world to bless other people day in and day out; we just need to look for a way to serve others.

In high school track, I was truly blessed with success. This picture was taken at the Crest relays as I finished the 440-yard dash. That night, I won the 440-yard dash and anchored the winning mile relay team.

I was told by my track team members they could tell if I was going to win when I started to smile on the backstretch going into turn three. I would start to smile and pick up my pace by leaning into the curve and running even harder. My mother's pride and my accomplishments came out the most when I ran. Her friends have shared with me and laughed with her that when I ran in track, no one dared stand too close to her. Her arms mimicked my arms as I ran, and even her feet at times would stomp up and down in coordination with my pace. Most of her friends or spectators would move away. She was so animated that I am not sure who was more exhausted her or me when the race was over. She would always have a tremendous smile on her face that I could see from the tracks. My Dad, on the other hand, would normally see me after the track meet or the next day and simply place a hand on the shoulders and say, "I am proud of the work you put in; you paid the price to be a winner." So, the smile came back, and the joy in running came back, but I have never been able to regain the belly laugh my mother so loved.

Swimming was another sport I loved and was able to win in the butterfly and individual medley. Summer brought Southwest Iowa City Swimming League and AAU Midwest Swimming Meets that kept me busy all summer. I will never forget the members of the swim team that I competed with or coached. Swimming was no longer a therapy for me. It was something that I enjoyed participating in and a major part of my life through high school and college. This love of swimming carried me into my next job. I became a Red Cross swimming instructor and swimming coach. I lived at the city pool every summer for years. I was a lifeguard, worked in the filter room, and was a boating and canoeing instructor. The Red Cross hired me as the summer swimming director. I also was hired by the city to be the city swimming pool manager. I owe any of my success to a gift from our Lord—unbelievable good memories of my home town and growing up in that community.

In my freshman year in high school, I was attending three other churches with friends of our family and asking questions on the many differences in the services and practices because I was just inquisitive. Mom and Dad encouraged me to go with our close friends' children to church services if they invited me. All three of my friends would also come with me when I invited them to church. When I was visiting, I would even talk with one of the ministers and all three Sunday school teachers about the differences in doctrinal teaching. Sometimes, the adults or the one minister was very open and enjoyed my questioning, but a few times, one was very uncomfortable to the point I stopped asking questions. I never wanted to make someone nervous or ill at ease when I was just wanting to know more about doctrine for my own understanding.

I started church hopping and had attended five different denominations with a desire to understand each church doctrine when I was invited by a classmate to Sunday evening church. She lived her values first by being humble and at the same time being an example of her Christian values at school. I was also invited back to Wednesday evening church services by one of the guys at school

A MIRACLE

who was also a classmate after he saw me in Sunday evening service. The thing that drew me to this church community was they lived their Christian values at church, in school, after school, and in school activities. A Christian life that is godlike attracts other people to the Lord. I wanted to be part of that consistency in my life, and I wanted to find God's plan for me. My parents had always stressed that God had a plan for me when I was struggling through polio, and I wanted to answer that plan. My classmates in this church community openly talked about their desire to serve God and at the same time were sensitive and humble while understanding others may not yet be ready to take on those responsibilities. They weren't afraid to say I know Jesus mostly in actions but also wanted to share the good news. I felt like I belonged here, and I started attending all the services. You know you are home when you have a spot in the pews that other members look for you to be setting in for each service.

During my freshman year in high school, I knew of God but didn't personally know God even though I was raised in the church. I didn't understand God's grace; I didn't understand that he would allow Jesus to pay the price on that rugged cross for me. The message that God loved me and that the price Jesus paid was for me was during a Wednesday evening service. I was moved by the Holy Spirit, and I accepted our Lord as my personal savior. I came forward during the invitation, and that decision changed my life. It took away the anger and mistrust and granted me peace. The hymns that we sang—"Trust and Obey," "The Old Rugged Cross," and "Just as I am Without One Plea"—still bring back memories of that invitation and of the pastor who spent time with me one-on-one as I grew in the Word. In our one-on-one time, my pastor stressed the importance of memorizing scripture that brought back memories from my earlier years. When we put his words in our hearts, the Holy Spirit can be present in our thoughts.

> My son, if you receive my word, and treasure my commandments within you, so that you incline your ear to wisdom and apply your heart to understanding; Yes, if you cry out for discern-

> ment and lift up your voice for understanding, if you seek her as silver and search for her as for hidden treasures, then you will understand the fear of the Lord and find the knowledge of God.
> —Proverbs 2:1–5 (NKJV)

I didn't have to do anything for this gift; it was given to me. I was so thankful for being invited to attend church that evening by a friend. This was a defining moment in my life that would change my goals for the rest of my journey. Adult and youth members of my now new church completely accepted me.

God never meant us to travel on our life's path alone. That is what Paul meant when he wrote, "I can do all things through Christ who strengthens me" (Philippians 4:13 NKJV). He is our partner in everything if we look for him. My new church community also believed that God was with us and showed that to me. I now had new duties to pray regularly, to study God's word, to let God's light shine, and to rejoice in the Lord. Did I mess up? Yes, but I tried to improve each day. I felt the challenge to be a blessing to others. Again, I have messed up, but I have always returned to that challenge and tried to improve. Mom and Dad encouraged me to be independent and trusted my judgment on where I wanted to attend church. When God touches the heart of a believer, he takes us to new places we could never reach on our own. I understood this new life gave to me my new nature in Christ.

> Whoever drinks of this water will thirst again, but whoever drinks of the water that I shall give him will never thirst. But the water I shall give him will become in him a fountain of water springing up into everlasting life.
> —John 4:13–14 (NKJV)

I learned in going through physical therapy and in athletics that your attitude and setting goals would lead to improvement and eventually success. I took this lesson and applied it to my Bible studies at home and in church. Saturday night was a time to read the lesson and prepare for Sunday. Sunday night was a time to enjoy songs and lift up our voices to the Lord—what a blessing. Wednesday evenings were a time to gather and, by gathering, support each other with our presence in the church.

> Again I say to you that if two of you agree on earth concerning anything that they ask, it will be done for them by My Father in heaven. For where two or three are gathered together in MY name, I am there in the midst of them.
> —Matthew 18:19–20 (NKJV)

Mom would stay with Dad and listen to the Sunday sermon from my new church on the radio from time to time and ask me questions about the sermon. This reminded me of when I was a child in elementary school; Mom would ask me questions about my Sunday school lesson on our way home from church. That gave me a great feeling and great memories of my childhood. Dad told me as long as I felt that God was present in the church, he was okay with my new church community and never brought it up again. Dad was very private in his faith. He would wake up early, make coffee, and go to a quiet place to enjoy the morning. I watched him through the kitchen window in good weather go to the back porch with his coffee in hand and his thoughts. He would sit in the corner of the porch and lower his head, which looked like he was talking to himself. I soon realized he was in prayer. He always ended this time by looking up, smiling, and coming back into the house. He never admitted he was in prayer. He usually said he enjoyed the time drinking his coffee without any interruptions.

> But you, when you pray, go into your room, and when you have shut your door, pray to your Father who is in the secret place, and your Father who sees in secret will reward you openly.
> —Matthew 6:6 (NKJV)

I did mimic Dad in his prayer time now that I understood the need to spend time with God. I started each day early with reading time in my Bible and followed it by asking God to allow me to understand his word or to use me in some small way. The Bible readings were given to me by my pastor and helped me understand my new role. Because I was involved in high school athletics, many of the younger children at church and some of the high school students too looked up to me. Another duty was to be concerned about how others saw me.

> Abstain from every form of evil.
> —1 Thessalonians 5:22 (NKJV)

I did try to act in a way to build up other's faith or even someone outside the church to believe in Jesus Christ. I did fail at times but have kept this ever-present in my mind and have worked so hard to do so. My success in track gave me the responsibility to not be a stumbling block to others.

> Or do you not know that your body is the temple of the Holy Spirit who is in you, whom you have from God, and you are not your own? For you were bought at a price; therefore, glorify God in your body and in your spirit, which are God's.
> —1 Corinthians 6:19–20 (NKJV)

I invited Dad to attend church with me once, and he shared with me the story of the pharisee and the tax collector.

> Two men went up to the temple to pray, one a Pharisee and the other a tax collector. The Pharisee stood and prayed thus with himself, "God, I thank you that I am not like other men—extortioners, unjust, adulterers, or even as this tax collector. I fast twice a week; I give

> tithes of all that I possess." And the tax collector, standing afar, would not so much as raise his eyes to heaven, but beat his breast saying, "God, be merciful to me a sinner!" I tell you this man went down to his house justified rather than the other; for everyone to exalts himself will be humbled, and he who humbles himself will be exalted.
> —Luke 18:10–14 (NKJV)

He explained to me he never wanted to be a pharisee by attending church and that his faith was private. Dad was also the one that encouraged me in school partially through his love of learning and his ability to sit with me while I read assignments. He helped me greatly and shortened my reading time by picking out the details in the textbook. I believed he recognized my reading problem but never spoke about it. He demonstrated his love of learning by reading history and science books just to see what was in them. He would later share facts from his reading that he enjoyed knowing. Dad never stopped reading my science books all the way through high school and college. There were times in college we got into very deep discussions on the details of plant physiology in my botany book. Dad made learning fun by the smile on his face when he helped me with lessons or we simply discussed something in a textbook. Dad was raised at a time when men were never emotional, so he didn't show or share his feelings.

Men were strong and quiet and did the right thing for the family and country and didn't expect any rewards or even a thank-you from others. His emotions were a smile directed at me as he would place his hand on my shoulder and then squeeze with a slight shaking motion. That was it, and I understood and loved it when he did that. We never spoke the words, but I accepted the smiles between us. He never told me verbally he was proud of me. He would say he was proud of the work I put in or proud of what I accomplished. He never said that he was proud of me in those words and only said that he loved me once in his life.

It was a few days before he passed away after he had been revived when his heart stopped. He looked at me and said that he guessed it was time to go. He looked directly at me and said, "I love you, Steve." I placed my hand on his shoulder and squeezed as I said, "I love you, Dad." He passed away a few days later. I am so glad we spoke those words to each other. Although we knew we loved each other, we didn't express it outside of the smile. I was much like my father with my sons but have tried to say "I love you" verbally to them. I pray that as a father, I have shared those words. I believe because of the care and support of adults as I grew up, I wanted to be involved in the ministry, but my gift was teaching—another gift from God. I entered the field of education to be a teacher at the secondary level. That love of teaching was developed early as a Red Cross swimming instructor. Who would have known that the therapy of swimming would develop into a gift of service to others in education? My first job after college was in a handicapped center in Northern Iowa as a teacher. Swimming therapy at the handicapped center was a major part of my job. I also found a great church to be part of because of two parents of my students at the center. The gift of teaching placed me in an education career and has been so rewarding for me over the years.

> If then you were raised with Christ, seek those things which are above, where Christ is, sitting at the right hand of God. Set your mind on things above, not on things on the earth.
> —Colossians 3:1–2 (NKJV)

Chapter 13

Pneumonia

> Rejoicing in hope, patient in tribulation,
> continuing steadfastly in prayer.
> —Romans 12:12 (NKJV)

Once I was home, we found out that I was prone to many childhood diseases and pneumonia. I contracted the mumps, chicken pox, both forms of measles, scarlet fever, and rheumatic fever by being exposed to children at school that were infectious. In every case, I seemed to get the most severe form of the disease. This was due to a weakened immune system, and we found out many other polio survivors reflected the same symptoms of a weakened immune system. Dad would joke with me when I got sick and would tell me that if a job was worth doing, it was worth doing right and going the extra mile in doing it. He would smile and tell me not to do it when I got sick anymore.

The real threat to my health was pneumonia, which visited me regularly during the fall and winter. In the late fall, when the temperature started to cool down, Mom would always insist on dressing me in a hat, mittens, a scarf, and a heavy winter coat, which I had no say in but truly disliked it because none of the other students were dressing in full winter clothes at that point. My answer to this was to walk two blocks away from home on my way to school and stuff my scarf, mittens, hat, and sometimes heavy winter coat in the bushes of an elderly couple. It rained one day while I was in school; I was sure everything would be wet making it difficult to explain to Mom and Dad how it got wet. When I got to the hiding place in the bushes, my winter attire was missing. I looked all over and then heard a voice on the porch from the elderly couple's home. It was a smiling gentleman who asked me if I was looking for this as he held up my winter coat. I said that it was. He then said that he didn't want to see it get wet, smiled, and said that he would not tell on me to my parents. I am sure he had been watching me use the bushes on several other days that fall. Mom never learned about my hiding place, and I didn't use it again.

Pneumonia was a constant companion for me every winter resulting in hospitalization three times in elementary school, once in junior high, and once in high school. It would start in the fall after my immune system was run down from hay fever. A sore throat typically turned into strep throat, and it would advance to bronchitis and then to pneumonia. The doctors developed a treatment to break the pattern by sending me to the allergy specialist in Des Moines that successfully reduced the effects of the hay fever. They also started me on antibiotics at the end of the hay fever season to ward off the strep throat and bronchitis, which helped. Even with all these preventive steps, winter still resulted in walking pneumonia or pneumonia many times during the coming years. As a result of pneumonia, I developed scar tissue on my lungs that did and still does reduce my breathing capacity. Many of the bulbar polio patients that did survive fought the same problems with pneumonia. A few of the children that we stayed in contact with passed away from pneumonia in their teens.

In my case, by reducing my sensitivity to airborne pollen through allergy shots in Des Moines and using antibiotics as a preventive when early symptoms occurred, pneumonia became less and less of a threat to my life. Dealing with pneumonia was our first introduction to post-polio syndrome. Even with my success at recovering most of my strength and coordination and dealing with pneumonia, the doctors in Des Moines still cautioned my parents that my life expectancy would now be in my late thirties or early forties. They based this on historical data collected from other patients' lives and that their general health was poor and most of them passed away from other diseases early on. I never accepted that prediction and was so blessed because I was allowed to meet with the doctors when they met with my parents.

When I was in high school, Mom and Dad still loaded us up in the car and took me to the hospital for checkups, mostly for my lungs and heart. We would eat out and go shopping to make it a full day for the family. Mom changed her hairstyle, and Dad changed his also. They still encouraged me in everything I did. I was taller than Dad and my brother, which I loved to tease Dad about.

> The Lord will give strength to His people;
> The Lord will bless His people with peace.
> —Psalm 29:11 (NKJV)

The introduction of pneumonia vaccinations helped support my overall health. My primary care doctor and cardiologist are aware of my medical history and post-polio syndrome, so they have focused on preventive health care. This I am very thankful for and blessed with.

Chapter 14

Spiritual Gifts

> As each one has received a gift, minister it to one another,
> as good stewards of the manifold grace of God.
> —1 Peter 4:10 (NKJV)

Finding gifts for many seems to be easy. If you are talented in instrumental music or vocal music, you use that talent to perform. You may be talented at organizational skills, and you then organize activities, or you may be blessed with financial success, and your gift would be to donate funds to the church. I knew one very special person that their gift was making themselves available to transport children to and from church and to and from school activities and neighbors if they needed transportation. That was a gift that she made available to everyone around her. Some individuals are gifted with the power of speech and become preachers, while others serve in the missionary field. I stumbled over my gifts many times while walking the path to find that gift.

> Trust in the Lord with all your heart, and lean not on your own understanding; In all your ways, acknowledge Him, and He shall direct your paths.
> —Proverbs 3:5–6 (NKJV)

A MIRACLE

I needed an individual that stepped into my life and said I should teach because that was my skill. He was one of my instructors at Cedarville University in Ohio that sent me on my path of teaching. He asked me to substitute in a Bible Class for him at church that I realized I really enjoyed teaching. I am sure he planned that teaching experience to help me see where I belonged. I was encouraged by that instructor to major in education because of the feedback he received from the brief teaching role. Finding my gift meant trying and failing and that is my message to others. Keep trying till you find your place because you will in time.

Chapter 15

Post-Polio Syndrome

Cast your burden on the Lord, And He shall sustain you;
He shall never permit the righteous to be moved.
—Psalm 55:22 (NKJV)

The first time I heard about post-polio syndrome was the summer of my junior year in high school. A friend told me their parents were saying that those of us in Creston who had been hospitalized for long periods of time were going to see the paralyses return in a few more years. It wasn't referred to as post-polio syndrome, but it was what they were talking about. I was surprised to hear that because no one had ever told me that was a possibility for me. I am sure that my parents and doctors who treated me had hoped that post-polio syndrome would not be in my future.

I had improved far beyond any expectations. My parents may have not wanted to add the uncertainty of paralysis returning later in my life after all the work I had put in to recover from polio. I simply dismissed the possibility of paralysis from polio returning as it was only a rumor, and I went on with my life. During my freshman year in college, I had the opportunity to talk to a sport injury doctor because I had been injured in a workout. He asked me if I had any muscular problems or weaknesses that may have brought on the injury. I told him that I had been injured in high school in the same leg and that I also had polio as a child. He then discussed post-polio syndrome with me because in his previous practice he had treated several polio patients that had manifested the syndrome. He made an assumption that because I was competing in college athletics, I must have had a very mild case of polio as a child. He talked in detail about how the paralyses had returned to his patients in varying degrees. He also assured me since I had had such a mild case and had recovered so well that I probably would not suffer from post-polio syndrome down the road. I never disclosed to him how severe my case was but now knew I may have to deal with it down the road. I did appreciate the knowledge he shared with me on post-polio syndrome, but again, I went on with my life. I wasn't really ready to face post-polio syndrome yet, but I would in a few more years.

After my injury ended my participation in cross-country that year, two of my very good friends spent time in prayer with me. We were asking for his healing hands to guide me that year in school and church. The healing was given to me in personal Bible study time and church activities. I worked on memorizing scripture and supporting youth activities of the younger children at church. Leading children in Bible study time helped me study and grow each week. God had a plan to put me in a leadership position of our youth, which strengthens my belief in the scriptures.

> All Scripture is given by inspiration by God and is profitable for doctrine, for reproof, for correction, for instruction in righteousness, that the man of God may be complete, thoroughly equipped for every good work.
> —2 Timothy 3:16–17 (NKJV)

Post-polio syndrome has been detected in many polio survivors and has reminded us that it did more damage than anyone knew. It is now showing up as muscle weakness, fatigue, joint pain, and shaking limbs in many adults that had polio in the '50s. Most of us would contract diseases that had polio-like symptoms. Muscle atrophy and breathing and swallowing problems have returned for those of us that had been treated in the iron lungs along with generally poor health.

I have lost one-third of my lung capacity, which has caused me to breathe more controlled over the years. Because of this, I am no longer able to even sing in church; I lack lung capacity. If I try, I will become very dizzy much like when I was working on exhaling as a child in the hospital. My symptoms are minor as compared to others that I know of. They have had to struggle with very severe conditions, and some have passed away. Again, for those of us treated in an iron lung, diseases such as asthma, COPD, or even a shrinking throat and swallowing problems would be in our lives early on that may or may not be post-polio syndrome. I was diagnosed with asthma in the third grade and have received treatments ever since. The treatments have helped somewhat because it's not really asthma but very similar. It has been more and more difficult to treat in the past few years. I have had to have my throat stretched several times to help due to weakening muscles in that area that has given me swallowing problems. This is a common procedure and easy to receive. Post-polio syndrome individuals simply suffered from very poor health in many areas.

From time to time, I have a numbness in one or both legs. It is enough in severity; I am not stable, so I must use a cane or canes to keep from wobbling. It comes and goes; I have had long periods of no problems with my walking and other times with no warning back on a cane. I have controlled it by using isometric exercises when the weakness comes on. Although it has visited suddenly and without any warning causing me to need help getting up or walking without a limp, other times, it comes on slowly, and I can start my exercises to prevent the numbness. Connie has been able to pick up on my walking gate and help me walk or rise when it visits suddenly. She has also been able to detect it before me at times and will warn me it is happening. I can walk fine by using mild exercising to my legs regularly much the same as I did when I was improving as a youth. So, now, targeted exercises for my legs are back in my life, which allows me to walk fine and without the help of a cane. I am in a period of no problem; right now, that has lasted over seventeen months. Fatigue seems to be a trigger that starts the wobbling, and rest seems to help at first to relieve the wobbling. I also have found that I must stretch my hands to keep them from shaking. The shaking is more pronounced in my left hand than in my right hand. My left hand will tighten up and cause me to not be able to open it without regularly exercising it. The hand exercises are easy to do at any time or any place, so this is not difficult or a major change in my life. I simply open and close my hands and grip something handy, and that helps. I am so blessed that this muscle weakness and shaking are manageable.

Another old friend has come back to visit me—eye tracking. My eyes will jerk and lose my place on the page when I become tired or have been reading too much. The good thing is that I no longer have to read, and I only do it for enjoyment, so I can stop anytime and come back to it the next day.

> My flesh and my heart fail, but God is the strength of my heart and my portion forever.
> —Psalm 73:26 (NKJV)

Many post-polio syndrome individuals have not been able to cope with the symptoms because they have been so severe that they no longer are with us. My heart condition was brought on by an enlarged heart, which was common in bulbar polio children and contributed to many early deaths.

In the '70s, I reacted to the early symptoms by exercising because I thought it was the lack of activity or it was just my age. When I realized it was more than the lack of activity, I was working in the family feedstore loading and unloading feed from boxcars into our warehouse on trucks for delivery. I would come home with the shakes and even have to breathe very shallow to control my breathing.

My wife was a gift that supported me through these symptoms of post-polio syndrome. She is truly a pearl of great price. If you look for miracles and/or blessings in everything and every day, you will see them. I worked through it with the help of my wife and what I call controlled breathing. Early on, doctors thought I may be in the early stages of Parkinson, but again, it was determined it was post-polio syndrome, not Parkinson. I am careful not to get fatigued now because when I do, mild shaking comes back to my hands and lower legs.

When I returned to the classroom as a teacher and later to school administration, some of the problems subsided because I could better manage my physical demands and control fatigue. The joint pain is ever-present and seems to be constant in my life. The symptoms are so far manageable, and I'm thankful for that. Faith gives us hope, and hope allows us to push ahead so we can open our hearts to God. I have been asked by an individual how I keep hope while facing post-polio syndrome. I have found hope by serving the Christian community as a Stephen Minister and a hospice chaplain, which allowed me to support others in times of need. The strength and actions of the individuals who maintained their Christian testimony even though they were going through personal trials and in many cases in their final days here on earth gave me strength. I saw their hope that there is a place prepared for them next to our Lord. That hope gives me hope every day and renews my belief in hope.

I remember an elderly person receiving hospice benefits that in her final days wanting to pray for me because she was concerned that I spent most of my days serving others and I would become depressed. We had spent time reading the Bible together and praying for wisdom. After our prayer, I usually would thank her for the time we spent together and tell her I would see her in a few more days. That day, she stopped me from leaving and said, "I want to pray for you." What a blessing that was for me and what an example of how I would want to spend my final days caring for others. That is where I find hope in facing post-polio syndrome; it is given to me through the lives of fellow Christians. Caring for others is the greatest task we can take on. Being able to do this gives me strength because I can see God working in the lives of others. Hope anchors my soul and gives me strength when I am worn out.

> Therefore, my heart is glad, and my glory rejoices; My flesh also will rest in hope.
> —Psalm 16:9 (NKJV)

My major problem has been the damage that polio apparently did to my heart. Early on, when I was still being checked on in follow-up appointments at Blank Children's Hospital, it was known that my heart was enlarged and that it may or may not be a problem into adulthood as no one really knew. My first real episode of chest pain was misdiagnosed as stress, and six years went by with me accepting the chest pain as stress. Shortly thereafter, the chest pain increased and resulted in a heart attack that sent me to the hospital for surgery. All of my cardiologists have concurred that my heart problems were never stress but mild heart attacks. The early damages weakened my heart and caused my heart attack, which was a result of polio. I was a superintendent of schools in a consolidated school system of five rural school districts at that time. I was so blessed with an administrative team that worked so hard during my hospitalization and an understanding school board. They checked on Connie and me almost daily, which helped us through the rehabilitation. I retired from my position as a public school superintendent and took a position as a superintendent of a Christian school district in Iowa. I was privileged to help the district to become certified through the Iowa Department of Education and able to teach a few classes at the twelfth-grade level. I was also able to help write the curriculum documents to maintain our Christian values and still meet the state's education requirements. That gave me hope that I could still serve children and our Lord. It showed me that I had value for others and still able to serve the Christian community.

> That you may walk worthy of the Lord,
> fully pleasing Him, being fruitful in every good
> work and increasing in the knowledge of God.
> —Colossians 1:10 (NKJV)

What a blessing that God granted in allowing me to know the staff and the families associated with that school. My health declined enough that I had to leave the school and retire again with a new diagnosis that I had only a year left to live. Connie and I decided that she need to be with our children for support if the diagnosis was correct. We moved to Dallas, Texas, and found new hope with a new surgeon that was willing to attempt a second surgery that was successful. He was a person that wanted me to pray for him because he felt that God always has a role to play in our lives. He didn't ask that of everyone, only if he was aware that they were Christians. I have returned to many of the exercises of the past to work through this post-polio syndrome. I have had three surgical heart procedures that have improved my quality of life. After my second procedure, I improved enough that I could again return to the classroom in a Christian environment in McKinney, Texas. I was so honored to be able to again teach biology but most of all to high school Christian students and see the knowledge and strength they had in our Lord.

> Now, may the God of hope fill you with all
> joy and peace in believing that you may abound
> in hope by the power of the Holy Spirit.
> —Romans 15:13 (NKJV)

As my years now creep up, I am still dealing with additional heart problems but have been able to stay ahead of them and even accomplished some positive rehabilitation of my heart with my present cardiologist. I now must use oxygen at night because my breathing has returned to being very shallow at night, but oxygen therapy has controlled it. Post-polio syndrome lingers in many of the survivors of polio, and we have recognized it and learned what medical treatments support our problems. There are very few people left that understand what the survivors of polio went through. The powerless feeling that we had from being partially paralyzed or in some cases totally paralyzed and unable to even breathe was only overcome by the support of everyone around us. For a child that was given less than a ten-percent chance of surviving, none of my problems from post-polio syndrome have been unmanageable, and because of this, my life has been filled with many blessings from the medical field over the years.

> The glory of young men is their strength,
> and the splendor of old men is their gray head.
> —Proverbs 20:29 (NKJV)

A MIRACLE

I do believe that the extensive therapy and work I put in with the support of my parents and my brother led to my success in athletics is the very reason post-polio syndrome is manageable now in my life. I am so thankful that I was encouraged to keep working and improving over the years. I trusted that God knew my destiny and prepared the way. Any of my accomplishments were his plan. He worked through my family and the church to support my recovery.

> Train up a child in the way he should go,
> and when he is old, he will not depart from it.
> —Proverbs 22:6 (NKJV)

Connie and I have hope because we have a personal relationship with our Lord and Savior Jesus Christ.

Chapter 16

Caregivers

A new commandment I give to you, that you love one another; as I have loved you, that you also love one another.
—John 13:34 (NKJV)

I wish I could have told this story day by day. I wish I could have remembered the children that bobbed up and down in the hot baths better or the other children that would lay in pain on the exercise tables with me and the tears we shared in pain for each other, but my memories are blurred or just not there, while other memories are seared visibly and distinctly as they were yesterday. So, I shared what I remembered or what I was told by my parents growing up and my brother that helped fill in some of the stories. Putting my memories to words brought back sadness, very deep sadness, to the point that I stopped writing my memories at times. I had willingly forgotten many memories of sadness, but writing these memories also brought back the joy of my family and God's hand in all of this. We as believers find our true identity the closer we move to God in life's journey.

I wanted to share my belief that miracles are real and still happen in this world; we only need to look for them. I firmly believe that God does put people in the right place at the right time to accomplish miracles. God worked through people to perform miracles in the past and still does today. I wanted to thank my parents for the unwavering support in allowing me to try—to struggle through the difficult trials because they felt the pain in everything I went through. They never let me forget that God had a plan for all of his children. None of the doctors, nurses, and therapists that served us at a time knew how polio was transmitted, but they were there to serve us putting themselves at risk. I grew up at a great time in the nation's history and even in a greater community. Creston had and still has outstanding people who truly supported me growing up, both adults and my classmates. I was so privileged to be part of that community.

My parents lived through the Great Depression and World War II and were part of "the greatest generation ever"—they sure were to me. Thank you for being great parents!

> And let us not grow weary while doing good, for in due season we shall reap if we do not lose heart. Therefore, as we have opportunity, let us do good to all, especially to those who are of the household of faith.
> —Galatians 6:9–10 (NKJV)

THERE IS ALWAYS HOPE

For You are my hope, O Lord God; You are my trust from my youth.

—Psalm 71:5 (NKJV)

Resources

Des Moines Sunday Register, Des Moines, Iowa, January 28, 2007
History of Polio, Wikipedia, The Free Encyclopedia
Photos retrieved from my mother's photo box from her estate
New King James Version (NKJV). Thomas Nelson, Inc., 1982.

About the Author

Steven Clark is a retired public school superintendent and a headmaster/superintendent of schools in the private sector after retiring from public schools. Steven served on numerous educational advisory boards at the state level in Iowa. He also chaired the Superintendent's Council in his local educational area in Iowa and was chairman of the Foster Care Review Board at a county level. Steven received the Iowa Governor's Volunteer Award and was elected as Superintendent of the Year for the Green Valley Area Education Agency in Iowa. Steven and his wife have been married for fifty years and reside in North Texas. They have three married sons and ten grandchildren. They are actively involved in small church groups and presently lead a senior citizens group for social activities and Bible study. Steven has served the Lord's Supper to those in nursing homes and home-bound individuals. He presently serves as a Stephen Minister and a lay speaker and has also served as a hospice chaplain in the areas of Dallas and McKinney, Texas.

CPSIA information can be obtained
at www.ICGtesting.com
Printed in the USA
BVHW060846040521
606331BV00018BA/1790